United States Virgin Islands History, a Travel Guide

The Journey to the Island, Inhabitant's. Root, Culture and tradition.

Author

Tyler Simpson

Copyright © 2018.
First Printed: 2018.

Carré 1957 Zogbo Littoral
Cotonou JB, 1015.

Table of Content

The Record

In 1493, Christopher Columbus landed on an island he named Santa Cruz. Driven away by the Carib Indians, he sailed northward to a nearby group of islands he called Las Once Mil Virgenes, in honor of Saint Ursula. The French took Santa Cruz from Spain in 1650, renaming it Saint Croix. The towns of Christiansted and Frederiksted on Saint Croix and Charlotte Amalie, the capital, on Saint Thomas were founded by the Danes and named after Danish royalty.

United States Virgin Islands, also called U.S. Virgin Islands, organized unincorporated island territory of the United States, situated at the eastern end of the Greater Antilles, about 40 miles (64 km) east of Puerto Rico, in the northeastern Caribbean Sea. It is composed of three large islands St. Croix, St. John, and St. Thomas and about 50 small islets and cays. The capital is Charlotte Amalie, on St. Thomas.

Demography. In 1999, the population was estimated at 120,000. The main population groups are West Indian (74 percent born in the Virgin Island,s and 29 percent born elsewhere), United States mainland (13 percent), Puerto Rican (5 percent) and others (8 percent). Blacks constitute 80 percent of the population, whites 15 percent, and others 5 percent.

Location and Geography

Geologically, with the British Virgin Islands, the U.S. Virgin Islands are an extension of the central fault-block mountain ranges of Puerto Rico and are thus part of the Greater Antilles. They are composed of metamorphosed igneous and sedimentary rocks overlain in parts by limestone and alluvium, and they rise off the continental shelf to maximum heights of 1,556 feet (474 metres) at Crown Mountain on St. Thomas, 1,277 feet (389 metres) at Bordeaux Mountain on St. John, and 1,088 feet (332 metres) at Mount Eagle on St. Croix—the largest of the islands, with an area of 84 square miles (218 square km). St. Thomas and St. John are very rugged, but St. Croix's mountains are confined to the north, with a large rolling-to-level plain opening to the south. All the islands are surrounded by fringing coral reefs, and ancient elevated reefs ring the main islands.

Linguistic Affiliation. English is the official language. A Dutch Creole, Negerhollands, arose in the seventeenth century on Saint Thomas from interactions between Dutch planters and African slaves and spread to Saint John and Saint Croix. In the next century, German missionaries translated the Bible into that language. With emancipation and the influx of English Creole speakers from other islands, the use of Dutch Creole declined. An English Creole arose on Saint Croix and is still spoken, although its use is generally limited to older islanders. The United States takeover in 1917 resulted in American English becoming the standard administrative, educational, and economic language. "Virgin Islands English," which retains some Creole features, is widely used in personal and informal situations. Spanish has become increasingly important because of immigration from nearby islands; Spanish speakers make up 35 percent of the population of Saint Croix.

The climate is pleasant, with temperatures at St. Thomas averaging a maximum of about 82 °F (28 °C) during the day in January and 88

°F (31 °C) in July and being tempered throughout the year by northeasterly trade winds. Nighttime minimum temperatures are about 11 °F (6 °C) cooler, and the relative humidity is low for the tropics. Rainfall averages some 45 inches (1,100 mm) annually, with a marked rainy season from September to December. Droughts occur periodically, and hurricanes may strike the islands on rare occasions. Early plantation clearance destroyed the islands' tropical forest, which is now found only in a few places on St. Thomas and has elsewhere been replaced by secondary woodland and scrub. Island fauna is sparse, save for birds, but the surrounding seas abound in commercial and game species.

Symbolism. The territorial bird is the indigenous yellow breast, and the territorial flower is the yellow elder, commonly called "Ginger Thomas." The flag, adopted in 1921, is white with a yellow American eagle grasping three arrows in its left talon and with an olive branch in its right, between the blue initials "V" and "I." On its breast is a shield of the United States.

People, Tradition and Lifestyle

Ethnic Relations. The first elected black governor in the United States, Melvin Evans, took office in 1970. Relations between ethnic groups are generally good, although there has been some racial violence.

About three-fourths of the population is non-Hispanic black, a little more than one-tenth non-Hispanic white, and most of the remainder black or white Hispanic. Less than half of the population is native-born. English is the official language, but some French is spoken on St. Thomas, and Spanish is spoken on St. Croix among Puerto Rican immigrants. The population is predominantly Christian; Protestants constitute about half and Roman Catholics more than one-fourth of those professing a religion. The population increased rapidly in the mid- to late 20th century, primarily because of substantial immigration from the U.S. mainland, the eastern Caribbean, and Puerto Rico. The infant mortality rate is relatively low for the region, and life expectancy in years, in the mid-70s for males and the low 80s for females is about average. Charlotte Amalie, the largest settlement, is the only town with a population of more than 10,000.

Urbanism, Architecture, and the Use of Space

Several cultures have influenced local architecture. Wattle and daub construction, the use of cisterns to collect water, the "Big Yard" or common area, and verandas and porches can be traced to Africa. Danish culture is reflected in the design of towns, especially the "step streets"; street names; ovens and cookhouses; and red roofs. Yellow ballast brick, carried in ships from Europe, was used in construction along with locally quarried stone and coral. Open market areas, formerly the sites of slave markets, are found in the main towns. Many urban buildings date back to the colonial period.

Gender Roles and Statuses

Division of Labor by Gender. Women are increasing their participation in the economic and political areas. The U.S. Small Business Administration established the Virgin Islands Women's Business Center in 1999 to encourage and train women business owners. The heroine of the 1878 labor rebellion in Saint Croix was "Queen Mary," a canefield worker. The current Senate president and the presiding judge of the Territorial Court are women.

Marriage, Family, and Kinship

Marriage. One in three families is headed by a single female parent. The rate of unmarried teenage pregnancy is increasing and is a major social concern. Wedding customs range from the traditional African "jump the broom" to European-influenced church ceremonies.

Domestic Unit. According to 1995 census data, married couples comprise 57 percent of households and unmarried females with children, 34 percent. The average household has two children.

Inheritance. The concept of jointly owned "family land" accommodates the pattern of alternately settling down and moving that has characterized the lives of many families since colonial times.

The Arts and Humanities

Support for the Arts. A nine-member Arts Council and a thirteen-member Historic Preservation Commission are appointed by the governor. Community arts groups exist on all three islands, with private support from a number of sources.

Literature. The Caribbean Writer, sponsored by the University of the Virgin Islands, showcases local writers. Lezmore Emanuel, a folk composer and poet; the literary historians Adelbert Anduze and Marvin Williams; and the poets Gerwyn Todman, Cyril Creque, J. P. Gimenez, and J. Antonio Jarvis have all made significant contributions.

Graphic Arts. The most famous locally born painter, Camille Pissaro, was born on Saint Thomas but moved to Paris. A number of contemporary artists work outside the country. Tourist preference has influenced the development of visual arts; Caribbean themes predominate in local galleries, such as the Caribbean Museum Center on Saint Croix.

Arts & Crafts: The islands are home to many artists. Their work ranges from watercolor and oil paintings; to sculptures, wood-turning, hand-made jewelry and more. Look for local arts and crafts in galleries, shops, from vendors and at cultural events.

Art Classes: Some galleries, art centers and resorts offer art classes for adults and children. Most are for a couple hours and project based. Dropping in for a class can be a nice way to create a unique vacation souvenir; and mingle with residents.

Galleries: There are an assortment of art galleries on St. Thomas, St. Croix and St. John. Special art showcases, usually in the early evening, are common on weekends. There is a popular Art Walk once a month during season on St. Croix.

Performance Arts. Mocko Jumbie stilt dancers perform at festivals and celebrations. Mocko Jumbies are masked and wear straw hats with cutouts for the eyes and mouth. This clothing was traditionally a woman's dress, but long trousers have become an acceptable part of the costume. The figure symbolizes the spirit world, and so the entire body must be disguised. Small decorative mirrors are worn to indicate invisibility. The stilts give the dancer additional height to frighten away evil spirits and also allow the Mocko Jumbie to chase misbehaving children and to keep crowds back from parade routes.

The Reichhold Center for the Arts, the Island Center Theater, and the Caribbean Community Theater give dance, music, and theater performances. Groups such as the Saint Croix Heritage Dancers and the Caribbean Dance Company preserve and teach traditional folk dances, many with African roots. The traditional folk dance, the quadrille, dates back to eighteenth century European settlers.

There are groups that maintain traditional dances like quadrille and bamboula; as well as classical dance like ballet. Mocko jumbie troupes of stilt dancing are popular. There are musicians and bands that perform a variety of genres. Theater groups stage plays and musicals.

The State of the Physical and Social Sciences

The University of the Virgin Islands maintains an Agricultural Experiment Station, a Cooperative Extension Service, and the William P. MacLean Marine Science Center. Its Eastern Caribbean Center conducts social, survey, and environmental research. The Virgin Islands Ecological Research Station on Saint John provides support services for visiting scientists and students

Socialization

Infant Care. Women are responsible for infant care. Breast-feeding is supplemented by formula given in bottles; the use of formula results in early weaning. In more traditional households, folk beliefs about infant care, including the use of "bush tea" to induce sleep, are common.

Child Rearing and Education. A "bogeyman" is used as a threat to correct children's bad behavior. Education is compulsory and free. Multicultural education is seen as a necessity, but there is growing concern about the public schools, and those who can afford private schools generally choose that alternative. A higher percentage of females than males finish high school.

Higher Education. The University of the Virgin Islands, founded in 1962, has campuses on Saint Thomas and Saint Croix. It offers bachelor's degrees in a number of areas and master's degrees in business administration and public administration.

Etiquette
Politeness is considered important. Children are told to address adults as "sir" or "ma'am." Visitors are encouraged to smile, use greetings, and maintain a courteous attitude.

Religion
Religious Beliefs. The predominant religious affiliations are Baptist (42 percent), Catholic (34 percent), and Episcopalian (17 percent). Remnants of African culture are found in the belief in spirits.

Religious Practitioners. Under Danish rule, the Lutheran church was the state church; to practice any other religion, an official permit had to be granted. Permits were granted fairly easily, and sermons were not censored. With the coming of the Americans in 1917, the Catholic Redemptorists became the predominant religious order, and Catholicism was a major force through the 1940s, in terms of the influence which priests wielded over parishioners.

Rituals and Holy Places. Saint Thomas has the second oldest synagogue in the New World. Lord God of Sabaoth Lutheran Church and the Friedensthal Moravian Church on Saint Croix are the oldest congregations of their kind in the United States. To commemorate their freedom in 1848, former slaves built the All Saints Cathedral. The Arawak Indian carvings on Saint John may have religious significance.

Medicine and Health Care

There are hospitals on Saint Croix and Saint Thomas and a clinic on Saint John. Alternative healing methods are widely used, such as faith healing, chiropractic, and traditional "bush" remedies based on indigenous plants.

Secular Celebrations

Legal holidays include 1 January, New Year's Day; 6 January, Three Kings Day; 15 January, Martin Luther King Day; President's Day on the third Monday in February; Memorial Day on the last Monday in May; Independence Day, 4 July; Veterans Day, 11 November; and Thanksgiving.

Legal holidays commemorating local events include Transfer Day (from Denmark to the United States in 1917); 31 March, Organic Act Day; Virgin Islands/Danish West Indies Emancipation Day, 3 July; and D. Hamilton Jackson Day on 1 November. Carnival was officially reinstated in 1952 and is celebrated at different times. Carnival celebrations include parades, floats, stilt walking "Mocko Jumbies," steel pan competitions, beauty contests, and food fairs.

Social Stratification

Classes and Castes. Historically, the society was divided along caste and color lines. Even after emancipation in 1848, ex-slaves' participation in the political process was restricted and their freedom of movement and emigration were limited by legislation. A result of Danish determination to maintain the status quo was the Fireburn of 1878, a labor revolt on Saint Croix that destroyed many plantations.

Symbols of Social Stratification. The use of Standard English characterizes the upper classes. Children often use native forms at home and speak Standard English at school. A higher percentage of males speak dialect than do females. The use of dialect is considered an important part of the culture but an impediment to educational and economic mobility.

Economy and Food

The U.S. Virgin Islands economy is based primarily on tourism and other services. The leading sectors in employment are government service; trade, encompassing personal, business, and domestic services including tourism; manufacturing; and finance, real estate, and insurance.

About one-fifth of the total land area is farmland, most of it on St. Croix. In the late 20th century agricultural production underwent a transition from the traditional reliance on sugarcane to more-diversified crops. Fruits (especially mangoes, bananas, papayas, and avocados) and vegetables (notably tomatoes and cucumbers) are the main crops grown. Cattle (ranched on St. Croix), goats, sheep, and pigs are the main livestock. St. Croix produces milk sufficient for island needs. The government has built dams on St. Croix and St. Thomas to improve farmers' water supply. Only 6 percent of the land is forested, but the government has planted large areas of St. Croix with mahogany and has reforested parts of St. Thomas. A bay forest on St. John supplies leaves for the bay-rum industry. Fishing is restricted to supplying local needs and to sportfishing.

The islands have few domestic energy sources and thus rely on imported petroleum products to supply most of their needs, especially for electric-power generation. Solar energy plays a small but growing role in the territory's energy production.

Rum distilling was traditionally the islands' primary industry, but manufacturing eventually diversified to include petroleum refining, watch assembly, and the manufacture of chemicals, pharmaceuticals, and clothing. Petroleum refining ceased in 2012 with the closure of the HOVENSA plant on St. Croix after more than four decades in operation. The plant had been one of the world's largest such facilities and had produced most of the islands' fuel supply. The impact of its closure on the economy included substantial losses of jobs and revenue as well as the loss of its petroleum products. The U.S. government encourages industry by allowing certain manufactures to enter the United States duty-free, and the local government has offered tax incentives.

The adverse effects of the HOVENSA closure extended to the islands' imports and exports. Before the loss of the refinery, the primary import was crude petroleum (primarily from Venezuela) and the main export was refined petroleum (shipped mainly to the United States). Exports totaled more than four-fifths of imports in value annually. Other than petroleum, exports included clothing, watches, and rum, and the main imports were manufactured goods.

Tourism, based on the pleasant tropical climate, attractive scenery, good fishing, proximity to the U.S. mainland, and free-port status, dominates the economy. Virgin Islands National Park, covering some three-fifths of St. John, and Buck Island Reef National Monument, which includes all of the islet of Buck Island and the waters and coral reef surrounding it, are other major attractions. Souvenir and handicraft industries have developed for the tourist market.

The islands' extensive road network is mostly paved. St. Croix, St. John, and St. Thomas all have scheduled bus service. Charlotte Amalie, on St. Thomas, and Frederiksted and Limetree Bay, on St. Croix, are deepwater ports. A container port on the southern coast of St. Croix handles most of the islands' cargo traffic. There is ferry service between the three main islands and to the British Virgin Islands. There are two international airports, on St. Thomas and on St. Croix. Interisland seaplanes serve the islands and Puerto Rico, the British Virgin Islands, and Saint Martin.

Food in Daily Life. Cassava, pumpkins, and sweet potatoes are native to the islands, and a variety of seafood is found in the surrounding waters. Many recipes are based on African sources. Okra is an ingredient in killaloo, a stew with local greens and fish, and in fungi, a cornmeal-based side dish; conch appears in fritters, chowders, and mixed with rice. Guava, soursop, and mango are eaten, along with mamey and mesple.

Food Customs at Ceremonial Occasions. Sugar cakes made with coconut and boiled sugar, are a traditional midafternoon snack. Maubi, a local drink, is made from the bark of a tree, herbs, and yeast. Souse is a stew of pig's head, tail, and feet, flavored with lime juice that is served on festive occasions.

Basic Economy. Per capita income is high, but the cost of living is expensive and there is constant pressure for new jobs. A major economic problem at the beginning of 1997 was the high level of governmental debt; since that time, expenditures have been cut, revenues have been increased, and fiscal stability has been restored. An increase in the tax on rum is expected to increase revenues. The islands' lack of natural resources makes them dependent on imports for local consumption and later reexportation. The basic unit of currency is the U.S. dollar.

Commercial Activities. The retail sector, including hotels, bars, restaurants, and jewelry stores, accounts for nearly half of the islands' revenues. The service sector is the largest employer; a small but growing area is financial services. Construction increased after the hurricanes of 1995. Tourism is the primary economic activity, accounting for more than 70 percent of the gross-domestic product and 70 percent of employment. Around two million tourists visit the islands annually; two-thirds are cruiseship passengers, but air visitors account for the majority of tourism revenue. Agriculture has declined in importance.

Major Industries. Manufacturing consists of textile, electronics, pharmaceutical, and watch assembly plants. Saint Croix has one of the world's largest oil refineries and an aluminum smelter. The need to rebuild after hurricanes has caused an upsurge in the construction industry.

Trade. Imports include crude oil, food, consumer goods, and building materials. The major source of export revenue is refined petroleum, with manufactured goods contributing a significant amount. The major trading partners are the United States and Puerto Rico.

History

The first human habitation in the islands occurred as early as about 1000 bce, with the arrival of Arawakan-speaking people from the Orinoco River basin of South America. Primarily farmers and fishers, they began to settle in villages about 200 bce and eventually developed into the complex Taino culture beginning about 1200 ce. The warlike Carib settled in the islands in the mid-15th century and conquered the Taino. They were the islands' dominant culture by the time Christopher Columbus reached St. Croix in 1493. Columbus named the islands Santa Ursula y las once Mil Virgenes, in honour of the legendary St. Ursula and the 11,000 martyred virgins. In 1555 a Spanish expedition defeated the Carib and claimed the islands for Spain, but by 1625 English and French settlers were farming on St. Croix. In 1650 the Spaniards evicted the remaining English settlers, but the French took the islands later that same year. St. Croix was willed to the Hospitallers (Knights of Malta) in 1653, but they sold it to the French West India Company. In 1666 the English evicted the Dutch buccaneers who had established themselves on Tortola (now in the British Virgin Islands). That year Denmark claimed St. Thomas, and in 1684 it claimed St. John.

After dividing the islands into plantations, the Danes began growing sugarcane, first using convicted criminals and then, after 1673, African slaves for labour. Commerce developed from the triangular trade in slaves brought from Africa, rum and molasses sent to Europe, and European goods shipped back to the islands. St. Thomas became a major slave market for the Caribbean. Denmark purchased St. Croix in 1733, and it became a major centre of sugarcane production. U.S. statesman Alexander Hamilton was born on Nevis island in 1755 and taken to St. Croix in 1765, where he worked in a countinghouse.

By the early 19th century the sugar industry had begun to decline, and two slave revolts had shaken the plantation economy. Slavery was abolished in 1848, and in the 1860s the United States began negotiations to purchase the islands from Denmark. The sale was made in 1917 for $25 million. The islands were administered by the U.S. Navy until 1931, when they were transferred to the Department of the Interior; civilian governors appointed by the president then administered the islands. Tourism began to develop following the end of World War II in 1945.

In 1954 the Organic Act of the Virgin Islands was revised and became the basis for the islands' current governmental structure. In 1970 the first popularly elected governor took office, and in 1976 the islands were given the right to draft a constitution, subject to approval by the U.S. Congress and the president. A number of constitutional conventions took place over the following decades, but none of the drafts they produced achieved ratification. In 2007 a fifth convention was assembled, and in 2009 it submitted its draft to U.S. Pres. Barack Obama for consideration. The U.S. government returned it to the territory the following year with recommended changes, and in 2012 the convention began meeting again to discuss revisions to the document.

Emergence of the Nation. By 1600, the native population had been wiped out by the Spanish. The Dutch and English settled on Saint Croix, with the Dutch being driven out around 1645. The French and the Knights of Malta took possession from Spain; Denmark, which had established slave plantations on Saint Thomas and Saint John, purchased Saint Croix from France in 1733. Although Denmark suppressed the slave trade in 1803, the practice did not end until the British occupied the islands in 1807. The islands were returned to Denmark in 1815 and remained the Danish West Indies until their purchase by the United States in 1917. Originally under the control of the navy, they passed to the Department of the Interior in 1954.

National Identity. Many documents from the colonial period are in Denmark, not accessible to residents seeking to study the country's history. Since 1917, there has been a lot of migration to and from the islands to other parts of the Caribbean and to the mainland; until recently, less than half of the population was native-born. People emphasize the variety of cultures in the islands, and the advantage of being both "U.S." and "Caribbean."

More details History of USVI

Historians document that the first inhabitants, the Ciboneys, arrived on the islands during what is considered the Pre-Ceramic Culture. Arawaks were the next to arrive, establishing sites on St. John and St. Croix around 100 AD. Probably the best-known inhabitants, and those to arrive next, were the fierce Caribs and the more peaceful Tainos. Evidence of their time in the islands has been unearthed in recent years, and includes stone griddles, zemis (small carvings depicting the faces of their gods) and petroglyphs which are rock carvings visible on St. John's Reef Bay Trail.

The Caribs had taken control of St. Croix, then called Ay Ay, when Christopher Columbus sailed into Salt River on his second voyage in 1493, claiming the islands for Spain. The battle between the Indians and Columbus is considered the first insurgence in the New World. After renaming the island Santa Cruz, Columbus headed north where he spotted a chain of islands. He proclaimed they would be called Las Once Mil Virgenes (11,000 virgins) in honor of Ursula, martyred by the Huns for refusing to marry a pagan prince.

The demise of the islands' first residents, the Indians, was evident when the first Europeans after Columbus arrived in the late 1500s. Many countries expressed interest in the islands in the 1600s, including Holland, France, England, Spain, Denmark and the Knights of Malta. But it was the Danes who established the first settlement on St. Thomas in 1672, expanding to St. John in 1694. St. Croix was added to the Danish West India Company in 1733, and plantations soon sprung up all over the islands.

Slave Trade and Piracy

In 1685, the Danish government signed a treaty with the Dutch of Brandenburg. This treaty allowed the Brandenburg American Company to establish a slave-trading post on St. Thomas. Early governors also approved of St. Thomas becoming a pirates' safe haven. The governors realized an influx of pirates would benefit local merchants. While piracy ceased to be a factor in the island's economy in the early 1800s, the slave trade continued.

In the Danish West Indies slaves labored mainly on sugar plantations. Cotton, indigo and other crops were also grown. Sugar mills and plantations dotted the islands hilly landscapes. Each islands economy prospered through sugar plantations and slave trading. While St. John and St. Croix maintained a plantation economy, St. Thomas developed into a prosperous center of trade. Slave rebellion on St. John and St. Croix are well documented. Legitimate trade and business on St. Thomas influenced a different society where many more slaves were given freedom and an opportunity outside of plantation life.

A July 2, 1848 rebellion on St. Croix, where some 5,000 blacks were free while another 17,000 remained enslaved, prompted liberal governor Peter von Scholten to declare what he had long pressed for, that all unfree in the Danish West Indies were from that day free. While his proclamation was in direct contradiction of the King's orders and while plantation owners refused to accept the proclamation, slavery was abolished on July 3rd, 1848.

Strict labor laws were implemented several times after emancipation and the populous reacted in tense labor riots.

Planters began to abandon their estates and the population and economy in the islands declined. The islands and its residents fell on rough times in the late 1800s due to the poor economy and numerous natural disasters.

US Territories

The islands remained under Danish rule until 1917, when the United States purchased them for $25 million in gold in an effort to improve military positioning during critical times of World War I. St. Croix, St. Thomas and St. John became the US Virgin Islands.

While conditions improved, change came slowly and frustrations brewed. Residents felt deceived when they were not granted American citizenship immediately following the transfer and disappointment also existed in that the islands were run by Naval administrators and appointed officials.

The Military and the Interior Departments managed the territory until the passage of the Organic Act in 1936. Today the USVI is a U.S. territory, run by an elected governor. The territory is under the jurisdiction of the president of the United States of America and residents are American citizens.

St. Thomas as a slave-trading post. More than 200,000 slaves, primarily from Africa's west coast, were forcibly shipped to the islands for the backbreaking work of harvesting cane, cotton and indigo. St. John and St. Croix maintained a plantation economy, while St. Thomas developed as a trade center. Stripped of their dignity and freedom and fed up with the harsh conditions, in 1733 slaves attacked St. John's Fort Frederiksvaern in Coral Bay, crippling operations for six months. In 1792 Denmark announced the cessation of the trade in humans. Freedom was not granted to slaves until 1848, when Moses "Buddhoe" Gottlieb led a revolution on St. Croix, 17 years before emancipation in the United States.

After the freeing of slaves and the discovery of the sugar beet, agriculture in the islands declined. The industrial revolution ended the need for the islands as a shipping port, thus changing the economic environment. Little was heard of the islands until World War I, when the United States realized their strategic position and negotiated the purchase of the islands from Denmark for $25 million in gold. Although the islands were purchased in 1917, it wasn't until 1927 that citizenship was granted to Virgin Islanders. The Organic Act of 1936 allowed for the creation of a senate, and from there the political process evolved. In 1970, the U.S. Virgin Islands elected its first governor, Melvin H. Evans.

Tourism grew in the destination once the United States imposed an embargo on Cuba in 1959. Today, the USVI is a thriving destination for visitors in search of the perfect vacation.

The period after Columbus' visit was quiet as far as exploration and colonization is concerned. Explorers as late as 1587 reported evidence of Indian habitation however settlers by 1625 reported not finding Indians. It is believed that Spanish settlers on nearby Puerto Rico raided the islands on a regular basis. Some Indians were forced to work while others fled. Indian groups lived throughout the Caribbean, however European exploration and colonization brought demise to the indigenous groups. They had no immunity to European diseases and were not prepared to deal with the harsh labor they were forced into. Within several decades following colonization of the Caribbean, Indian populations had plummeted. Today they are found on reserved lands on only a few islands. They no longer exist in what is today the USVI.

St. Thomas, St. Croix and St. John

In the early 1600s many countries took interest in the Caribbean and in "the Virgins"; Holland, France, England, Spain, Denmark and the Knights of Malta all sought colonies. England and Holland colonized and jointly inhabited St. Croix in the 1620s. The neighboring Spanish on Puerto Rico invaded the small colony; the French then quickly moved in, removing the Spanish and taking over themselves. St. Croix remained a French colony until 1733.

[The Danish West India Company first attempted to settle St. Thomas in 1665. They successfully established a settlement on St. Thomas in 1672 consisting of 113 inhabitants. They expanded and settled on St. John in 1694. The Danish had claimed St. John as early as the 1680's, however hostility from the neighboring British on Tortola prevented the Danes from establishing a settlement. The British, in order to maintain hospitable relations with Denmark, eventually ceased their opposition. After the Danes settled St. John plantation agriculture developed rapidly.

The Danish West Indian Company purchased St. Croix from the French in 1733 bringing St. Thomas, St. Croix and St. John together as the Danish West Indies.]

Discovery of St. Thomas: History

History

Population: 51,181 (2000 Census)

1. Charlotte Amalie (Town): 11,004
2. East End: 7,672
3. West End: 2,058
4. North Side: 8,712
5. Charlotte Amalie (Sub-district): 18,914
6. South Side: 5,467
7. Tutu: 8,197

8. **Size**: 31 square miles, 13 miles long and 4 miles wide
9. **Highest Point**: 1,556 feet – Crown Mountain

Archaeological evidence suggests that St. Thomas was once home to natives of the Ciboney tribes, the Taino or Arawak tribe and the Caribs. Indian habitation in what is today the Virgin Islands was recorded in journals kept by settlers and explorers in the late 1500s. By the 1600s however, the Indian populations had plummeted due to disease brought by Europeans, raids by Spanish settlers from neighboring islandsand immigration to other islands of the Caribbean. These indigenous groups no longer exists in the Virgin Islands.

Christopher Colombus is credited with "discovering" St. Thomas during his second voyage to the New World in 1493. He apparently was not impressed, as he didn't stay long, instead sailing on to Puerto Rico. The island was left unguarded by the Spanish and soon its sheltered bays were called on by ships from other nations, captained by men the Spanish would come to consider pirates. St. Thomas' existence would continue as home to pirates and small settlements long before a European power decided to pursue a permanent settlement.

In 1671 the Danish West India Company received its charter from King Christian V to occupy and take possession of St. Thomas and islands thereabouts that might be uninhabited and suitable for plantations. Part of the charter indicated that the Danish government would supply the company with as many male convicts as necessary for working the plantations andas many women, who were under arrest, as needed. Authorities would soon learn that convicts did not make good workers! The officials in St. Thomas would quickly welcome colonists from other neighboring islands and rely on African slaves for labor.

The first two ships that set sail to settle St. Thomas headed out on August 30, 1671 and arrived three months later on February 26,1672. The original crew included 116 men engaged by the company and 61 convicts. The first months and years of colonization were costly in terms of lives. Of the first two ships that sailed 89 people died on one ship and 75 died after landing. A third ship with 67 passengers on board sailed to St. Thomas in 1673; 7 died on board and 53 after landing! With these grim numbers the little Danish settlement on St. Thomas grew slowly. Many Dutch settlers seeped in from neighboring islands; consequently from the very beginning Dutch was the dominant language. In 1673 a ship of 103 slaves was sent to St. Thomas, another 24 added in 1675 and 16 in 1678. These were the first of many slaves brought to the island.

The population in 1680 was 156 whites and 175 blacks. The settlement included one fort, one road running through the island and about 50 plantations (of which 46 were occupied). Neighboring islands around St. Thomas, like Buck Island and Water Island, were used as pastures for goats and sheep; intended to feed the settlers on St. Thomas.

After some time passed the government realized that much of St. Thomas' future lay in the development of the area around the natural harbor. Soon Taphus was born! Taphus, meaning beer houses or halls, was the name of what is today Charlotte Amalie. The latter name used in honor of King Christian V's wife. When the governor gave licenses to residents to develop the area around the harbor, taverns quickly sprung up as did seafarers who enjoyed Taphus.

Seafarers... pirates! Under the Esmit Brothers, who served as the 2nd and 3rd governors of St. Thomas, the island gained the image of being a pirates den. This is not surprising considering the Esmit

Brothers are said to have illegally and openly traded with freebooters and allowed them to use St. Thomas as a refuge. Romanticized stories of piracy on St. Thomas are common; stories of pirates Blackbeard and Bluebeard are the most well known.

In 1685, after several years of poor management, the Danish West India Company signed a treaty with the Brandenburger Company allowing them to establish a slave trading business on St. Thomas. Despite the slave trade being big business, Bradenburger reports indicate that their prosperity was impeded by difficulties with the Danish hosts and conflicts with the Dutch West India Company.

The early 1700's were the boom period for St. Thomas, sugar became the popular crop and slave trading was on the rise. African slaves were used for labor on the many plantations that dotted the island. Additionally, many traders from other islands came to St. Thomas to buy slaves. Between 1691 and 1715 the population of St. Thomas grew from 389 whites to 547 and 555 blacks to 3042.

In 1717, a small group of planters, slaves and soldiers were sent from St. Thomas to claim St. John. And, on June 13,1733 the Danish West India Company bought St. Croix from France.

In 1754 a proposal recommending that the Danish Government take over the administration of the islands was approved by King Frederik V. The islands became crown colonies. Around this same time St. Croix was growing rapidly, its population almost doubling St. Thomas' and St. John's combined. The capital was moved from St. Thomas to Christiansted, St. Croix. While St. Croix developed a typical plantation economy, St. Thomas' economy shifted to trade.

The English seized the Danish islands in 1801 for about a year and again from 1807 to 1815. While the first takeover left little lasting effect the second caused trade on St. Thomas to stagnate and left some planters impoverished.

St. Thomas was made a free port in 1815 and in the years following it became a shipping center and distributing point for the West Indies. Charlotte Amalie flourished commercially. Large and small importing houses, belonging to English, French, German, Italian, American, Spanish, Sephardim and Danish owners, were thriving. A large part of all West Indian trade was channeled through the harbor. Of the 14,000 inhabitants, many of them free, only about 2,500 (mostly slaves) gained their living on plantations. A substantial segment of free Blacks worked as clerks, shop keepers and artisans. The population and atmosphere was very cosmopolitan, particularly in comparison to its sister island of St. Croix where plantation life was the norm. It is on St. Croix that a slave revolt in 1848 prompted the abolition of slavery in the Danish West Indies.

With the increase of steamships in the 1840's St. Thomas continued forward by becoming a coaling station for ships running between South and North America. Shipping lines made Charlotte Amalie their headquarters. Later advancements in steam and political climate made it possible for Spanish and English islands to import directly from producers, therefore skipping St. Thomas. By the 1860's the end of prosperity loomed in the horizon. Coaling however, would continue until about 1935. Coaling ships was an occupation largely filled by women.

In the late 1800s through early 1900s, several major natural disasters including hurricanes, fires and a tsunami left Charlotte Amalie wanting for major re-building. Years passed before the old warehouses that once stored goods for trade would be rebuilt to house the fancy boutiques and stores that line the streets today. On St. Croix, plantations were suffering with labor issues and low market prices on sugar. The Danish West Indies became more and more dependant on Denmark, and its treasury, during these difficult times.

Negotiations between the United States and Denmark were initiated on several occasions between 1865 and 1917 when the final deal was struck and the United States bought the Danish West Indies for $25 million.

The United States flag was hoisted on the three "Virgin Islands of America' on the 31st of March 1917. The islands remained under US Navy Rule until 1931; during that time several major public works and social reform projects were undertaken. Governors were appointed from 1931 until 1969 when the first elected governor took office. The capital of the island group is Charlotte Amalie, on St. Thomas.

As air and sea travel increased in the 1950s prosperity returned to Charlotte Amalie and St. Thomas. Tourism continued to grow in the years thereafter. The island saw an increase in population as immigrants from other Caribbean islands came in hopes of finding work in the developing tourism industry.

St. Thomas moved into the 21st century maintaining its prominence as one of the Caribbean's top vacation destinations and Charlotte Amalie as a favorite cruise ship port of call.

Charlotte Amalie, St. Thomas

St. Thomas is home to the capital of the U.S. Virgin Islands, Charlotte Amalie. It has been the heart of St. Thomas' activities from colonial times to present. Historic buildings found throughout downtown Charlotte Amalie take visitors back to the Danish era when the town was a bustling port of trade; while modern additions of taxis, shops, souvenir vendors and cruise ships in the harbor remind that it is tourism that currently drives the economy.

St. Thomas is largely mountainous. Many roads around the island offer terrific panoramic views of the island and ocean. Amongst the hills on St. Thomas and along the beaches you will find an assortment of accommodations; resorts, historic inns, guest houses, vacation homes, villas and condos.

St. Thomas is a water lover's paradise. For your vacation plan a few beach days, snorkeling, scuba diving, windsurfing, a day charter, kite boarding, sailing, fishing, kayaking and parasailing. On land you can play a round of golf, take an island tour, check out some attractions, take in the historical sites downtown and do some shopping. In the evening you can hit happy hour at a bar or restaurant, catch some live music and have dinner with a sublime view!

The Cyril E. King Airport serves travelers coming to St. Thomas. Visitors staying on St. John and Water Island can easily day trip to St. Thomas; daily ferry service is available. St. Thomas is connected to St. Croix by regular inter-island air service and a ferry.

Discovery of St John: History.

St. John, Virgin Islands

St. John is home to the **Virgin Islands National Park** which protects over 7000 acres of the 12,500 acre island. It offers visitors a unique opportunity to enjoy and appreciate the beautiful natural resources of the island. You can stay in an eco-friendly cabin or at a campground. At a beautiful resort or in villas and vacation rentals that range from quaint to super luxurious.

The resorts, vacation villas and homes for the 4000+ residents are found largely in and close to Cruz Bay and Coral Bay. Cruz Bay is the main town on St. John. It is the location of the ferry dock which connects St. John to St. Thomas. Cruz Bay has shops, grocery stores, a post office, schools, and so on. The second largest developed area Coral Bay also has restaurants, grocery stores and other businesses that cater to residents and visitors.

Population: 4,197 (2000 Census)
1. Central: 746
2. Coral Bay: 649
3. Cruz Bay: 2,743
4. East End: 59
5. **Size**: 20 square miles – 7 miles long, 3 miles wide
6. **Highest Point**: Bordeaux Mountain 1,277 ft

Archaeological evidence suggests that Indians inhabited St. John as early as 770 BC, however there were no lasting settlements until the 1720s. Attracted by the possibility of cultivating sugar cane for profit, several European countries laid claim to the little island around that time.

The British had claimed St. John when the Danish government took possession in 1684. Although the British had no settlement on St. John, residents on Tortola considered the island to be theirs. The first party of Danes that tried to settle St. John was asked to leave. The two countries disputed over ownership for some time.

On March 25th, 1718 a group of Danish planters from St. Thomas raised their flag at the first permanent settlement at Estate Carolina in Coral Bay. The group is said to have included 20 settlers. Coral Bay was not the finest area for planting but it had an excellent natural harbor. At this time the Danish colony on St. Thomas was well established and Danish and Dutch planters were excited by the prospects of establishing plantations on St. John.

The British continued their attempts to overtake the Danes on St. John, however in 1762, to keep good relations with the Danes they finally relinquished their claims. Expansion happened quickly. In 15 years approximately 109 cotton and sugar cane plantations covered almost all of St. John.

Plantation life

St. John's hilly terrain meant that it was a must that the hills be cleared and terraced. The soil became thin when the trees were cleared; this made it necessary to add ashes and dung to the soil to maintain fertility. Sugar cane had to be cultivated and processed. The growing number of plantations created a need for labor. It was not profitable to hire workers for the plantations. African slaves and indentured servants were brought to St. John to work the plantations. It was not long before the number of slaves on the island hugely outnumbered free-men.

Revolt of 1733

In 1733 there was a revolt on St. John against plantation owners and against slavery. On November 23rd, about 14 slaves entered Fortsberg with cane knives hidden in bundles of wood. They killed 6 out of 7 men in the garrison, took over the fort and fired one cannon to signal to the other slaves that the revolt had begun. The events that lead up to the revolt included; the adoption of a harsh slave code, the arrival of an elite group of African tribal rulers who preferred death to life as slaves and a summer of natural disasters, including a drought, two hurricanes, insect plaque and the possibility of famine. The seven month revolt left many Europeans and Africans dead. The recorded population at the time of the revolt was 1,295 – 1,087 slaves and 208 freemen. These figures do not include children under twelve or people who worked on company plantations in Coral Bay. The true population therefore was greater than 1,295. During the revolt almost a quarter of the island's population was killed and large plantations were destroyed. Many slaves killed themselves when they thought the soldiers were going to capture them. French and Swiss soldiers from a neighboring island came to the aid of the Danes and settled the revolt.

In 1825 the Danish government opened a new courthouse and prison in Cruz Bay. The structure was intended to improve the treatment of slaves on St. John, by making justice a government issue rather than leaving it to individual planters. This building is now known as the Battery and is the only government building from the Danish Colonial period that remains.

Slavery Abolished

The Danish Parliament around this time created a 12-year plan where slavery would be slowly dissolved. Many slaves said they would not wait 12 years. A revolt on St. Croix prompted Governor General Peter Von Scholten on July 3rd, 1848 to abandon the Parliament's plan and abolished slavery in the Danish West Indies.

With the end of slavery came the decline of St. John's plantations and a dramatic drop in population. Between 1850 and 1870 St. John is said to have lost half its population. The plantation at Carolina Estate was kept running the longest by use of bay oil and cattle, and the Reef Bay continued operation until 1919 as it had been converted to steam power. As sugar production became profitless, bankrupt planters abandoned the island and former slaves moved onto the land. Some bought the land, others were given land gifts from former owners and the remainder became squatters.

The main economy of St. John for many years following the decline of plantation life was small scale subsistence farming. The island saw prospects of renewed sugar economy when in the 1870's the possibility of producing cheaper sugar with beets was considered.

However this did not happen, as St. Croix and Puerto Rico were able to produce sugar more effectively and for less money. The island was left to the inhabitant that lived off the land and sea. Around 1913 the population of St. John is said to have been about 930 persons.

United States Virgin Islands

In 1917 the United States bought St. John from Denmark. By the 1930's, news of the beautiful American island had spread to the United States mainland and the beginning of what was to become a tourism boom on St. John was established.

Laurence Rockefeller in 1956 donated land to the Federal Government to establish a National Park. The 5000 acres became the nation's twenty-ninth National Park. The land was presented to Fred Seaton, who was the Secretary of the Interior, he promised the government would 'take good and proper care of these precious acres and verdant hills and valleys and miles of sunny, sandy shores'. Since then other donations have been made and presently the **Virgin Islands National Park** includes 7200 acres of land and 5600 acres of underwater lands.

Today St. John thrives as a favored tourist destination. A construction boom in the past couple of years is changing St. John from a quiet, sleepy island to one with a little more traffic and development.

Discovery of St Thamos: History

Population: 51,181 (2000 Census)

1. Charlotte Amalie (Town): 11,004
2. East End: 7,672
3. West End: 2,058

4. North Side: 8,712
5. Charlotte Amalie (Sub-district): 18,914
6. South Side: 5,467
7. Tutu: 8,197
8. Size: 31 square miles, 13 miles long and 4 miles wide
9. Highest Point: 1,556 feet – Crown Mountain

Archaeological evidence suggests that St. Thomas was once home to natives of the Ciboney tribes, the Taino or Arawak tribe and the Caribs. Indian habitation in what is today the Virgin Islands was recorded in journals kept by settlers and explorers in the late 1500s. By the 1600s however, the Indian populations had plummeted due to disease brought by Europeans, raids by Spanish settlers from neighboring islandsand immigration to other islands of the Caribbean. These indigenous groups no longer exists in the Virgin Islands.

Christopher Colombus is credited with "discovering" St. Thomas during his second voyage to the New World in 1493. He apparently was not impressed, as he didn't stay long, instead sailing on to Puerto Rico. The island was left unguarded by the Spanish and soon its sheltered bays were called on by ships from other nations, captained by men the Spanish would come to consider pirates. St. Thomas' existence would continue as home to pirates and small settlements long before a European power decided to pursue a permanent settlement.

In 1671 the Danish West India Company received its charter from King Christian V to occupy and take possession of St. Thomas and islands thereabouts that might be uninhabited and suitable for plantations. Part of the charter indicated that the Danish government would supply the company with as many male convicts as necessary for working the plantations andas many women, who were under arrest, as needed. Authorities would soon learn that convicts did not make good workers! The officials in St. Thomas would quickly welcome colonists from other neighboring islands and rely on African slaves for labor.

The first two ships that set sail to settle St. Thomas headed out on August 30, 1671 and arrived three months later on February 26,1672. The original crew included 116 men engaged by the company and 61 convicts. The first months and years of colonization were costly in terms of lives. Of the first two ships that sailed 89 people died on one ship and 75 died after landing. A third ship with 67 passengers on board sailed to St. Thomas in 1673; 7 died on board and 53 after landing! With these grim numbers the little Danish settlement on St. Thomas grew slowly. Many Dutch settlers seeped in from neighboring islands; consequently from the very beginning Dutch was the dominant language. In 1673 a ship of 103 slaves was sent to St. Thomas, another 24 added in 1675 and 16 in 1678. These were the first of many slaves brought to the island.

The population in 1680 was 156 whites and 175 blacks. The settlement included one fort, one road running through the island and about 50 plantations (of which 46 were occupied). Neighboring islands around St. Thomas, like Buck Island and Water Island, were used as pastures for goats and sheep; intended to feed the settlers on St. Thomas.

After some time passed the government realized that much of St. Thomas' future lay in the development of the area around the natural harbor. Soon Taphus was born! Taphus, meaning beer houses or halls, was the name of what is today Charlotte Amalie. The latter name used in honor of King Christian V's wife. When the governor gave licenses to residents to develop the area around the harbor, taverns quickly sprung up as did seafarers who enjoyed Taphus.

Seafarers... pirates! Under the Esmit Brothers, who served as the 2nd and 3rd governors of St. Thomas, the island gained the image of being a pirates den. This is not surprising considering the Esmit Brothers are said to have illegally and openly traded with freebooters and allowed them to use St. Thomas as a refuge. Romanticized stories of piracy on St. Thomas are common; stories of pirates Blackbeard and Bluebeard are the most well known.

In 1685, after several years of poor management, the Danish West India Company signed a treaty with the Brandenburger Company allowing them to establish a slave trading business on St. Thomas. Despite the slave trade being big business, Bradenburger reports indicate that their prosperity was impeded by difficulties with the Danish hosts and conflicts with the Dutch West India Company.

The early 1700's were the boom period for St. Thomas, sugar became the popular crop and slave trading was on the rise. African slaves were used for labor on the many plantations that dotted the island. Additionally, many traders from other islands came to St. Thomas to buy slaves. Between 1691 and 1715 the population of St. Thomas grew from 389 whites to 547 and 555 blacks to 3042.

In 1717, a small group of planters, slaves and soldiers were sent from St. Thomas to claim St. John. And, on June 13,1733 the Danish West India Company bought St. Croix from France.

In 1754 a proposal recommending that the Danish Government take over the administration of the islands was approved by King Frederik V. The islands became crown colonies. Around this same time St. Croix was growing rapidly, its population almost doubling St. Thomas' and St. John's combined. The capital was moved from

St. Thomas to Christiansted, St. Croix. While St. Croix developed a typical plantation economy, St. Thomas' economy shifted to trade.

The English seized the Danish islands in 1801 for about a year and again from 1807 to 1815. While the first takeover left little lasting effect the second caused trade on St. Thomas to stagnate and left some planters impoverished.

St. Thomas was made a free port in 1815 and in the years following it became a shipping center and distributing point for the West Indies. Charlotte Amalie flourished commercially. Large and small importing houses, belonging to English, French, German, Italian, American, Spanish, Sephardim and Danish owners, were thriving. A large part of all West Indian trade was channeled through the harbor. Of the 14,000 inhabitants, many of them free, only about 2,500 (mostly slaves) gained their living on plantations. A substantial segment of free Blacks worked as clerks, shop keepers and artisans. The population and atmosphere was very cosmopolitan, particularly in comparison to its sister island of St. Croix where plantation life was the norm. It is on St. Croix that a slave revolt in 1848 prompted the abolition of slavery in the Danish West Indies.

With the increase of steamships in the 1840's St. Thomas continued forward by becoming a coaling station for ships running between South and North America. Shipping lines made Charlotte Amalie their headquarters. Later advancements in steam and political climate made it possible for Spanish and English islands to import directly from producers, therefore skipping St. Thomas. By the 1860's the end of prosperity loomed in the horizon. Coaling however, would continue until about 1935. Coaling ships was an occupation largely filled by women.

In the late 1800s through early 1900s, several major natural disasters including hurricanes, fires and a tsunami left Charlotte Amalie wanting for major re-building. Years passed before the old warehouses that once stored goods for trade would be rebuilt to house the fancy boutiques and stores that line the streets today. On St. Croix, plantations were suffering with labor issues and low market prices on sugar. The Danish West Indies became more and more dependant on Denmark, and its treasury, during these difficult times.

Negotiations between the United States and Denmark were initiated on several occasions between 1865 and 1917 when the final deal was struck and the United States bought the Danish West Indies for $25 million.

The United States flag was hoisted on the three"Virgin Islands of America' on the 31st of March 1917. The islands remained under US Navy Rule until 1931; during that time several major public works and social reform projects were undertaken. Governors were appointed from 1931 until 1969 when the first elected governor took office. The capital of the island group is Charlotte Amalie, on St. Thomas.

As air and sea travel increased in the 1950s prosperity returned to Charlotte Amalie and St. Thomas. Tourism continued to grow in the years thereafter. The island saw an increase in population as immigrants from other Caribbean islands came in hopes of finding work in the developing tourism industry.

St. Thomas moved into the 21st century maintaining its prominence as one of the Caribbean's top vacation destinations and Charlotte Amalie as a favorite cruise ship port of call.

Government and society

The government is organized under the Organic Act of the Virgin Islands, passed by the U.S. Congress in 1936 and amended in 1954 and subsequently. The government has three branches: executive, legislative, and judicial. The governor, elected by universal adult (18 years and older) suffrage to a maximum of two consecutive four-year terms, appoints heads of the executive branches and administrative assistants for St. Croix and St. John with approval of the unicameral legislature. The 15 members of the legislature, called senators, are elected by universal suffrage to four-year terms. The people of the U.S. Virgin Islands are U.S. citizens, and they elect a nonvoting representative to the U.S. House of Representatives but do not vote in U.S. national elections. There are three political parties: the Democratic Party and the Republican Party, affiliated with the U.S. parties, and the Independent Citizens Movement. The District Court of the Virgin Islands operates under federal law and functions as a U.S. district court. The Superior Court is the court of first instance for many civil and criminal matters. Its decisions may be appealed to the Supreme Court of the Virgin Islands and, if necessary, taken for further review by a U.S. appellate court and, ultimately, by the U.S. Supreme Court.

St. Thomas and St. Croix have hospitals, and the public health service operates mobile medical units for outlying areas as well as a program for immunization, clinical services, home care services, and special programs. Education is compulsory for children to age 16 in public primary, secondary, and vocational schools. Higher education and teacher training are available at the University of the Virgin Islands (1962), a U.S. land-grant institution with campuses on St. Thomas and St. Croix. The main public library, located on St. Thomas, has branches on St. Croix and St. John. The Department of Planning and Natural Resources administers museum and library services.

Leadership and Political Officials. The current governor and the current representative to the U.S. House are both Democrats. In the Senate, the Democratic Party holds six seats and the Republican Party and the Independent Citizens Movement have two seats each; the remaining five seats are held by independents.

Social Problems and Control. The high cost of living and the low pay scale for service sector jobs have created widespread discontent. Saint Croix has seen drive-by shootings, but most crime is property-related. To protect tourism, the government has increased the law enforcement budget. Local officials work with the Drug Enforcement Agency, Customs, and the Coast Guard to combat the illegal drug trade.

Social Welfare and Change Programs
The Department of Human Services attempts to provide for the needs of low-income persons, the elderly, children and families, and the disabled.

Nongovernmental Organizations and Other Associations
The Saint Croix Foundation is active in community development and has established anticrime initiatives. Environmental associations on the three main islands promote ecological awareness, sponsor guided outings, and encourage responsible legislation.

Culture

Virgin Islands Culture

Caribbean and American that is a description of culture in the United States Virgin Islands. You will find fast-food restaurants like Subway and McDonalds next to local restaurants serving pates and boiled fish. You will find large grocery stores selling everything from Campbells Soup to Sara-lee pound cakes. Around the corner from the grocery store will be a fisherman selling a fresh catch from his truck. On the radio you can hear calypso music, reggae, American pop, salsa, blues, oldies, rock and roll and many other genres. Florida oranges and strawberries are sold as are kenips, mangos and coconuts. Fashions include jeans, t-shirts, jerseys, polo shirts and other Western style dress. Local sports enthusiast watch and play baseball, basketball and football. And CNN news is broadcasted daily and discussed just as often as local gossip. Together the American and Caribbean combination makes the United States Virgin Islands a unique and interesting place.

The population in the USVI is largely made up of Caribbean people whose ancestors were Africans and Europeans. You will find people from all across the Caribbean living in the Virgin Islands as well as Americans from the mainland, Europeans and Hispanics.

English is the main language in the USVI and the majority of the population speak, write and read English only. Some residents speak quickly and with an accent making it difficult to understand. Emigrants from other islands have brought other languages to the Virgin Islands therefore it is not uncommon to hear Spanish, French-Patois and Creole.

Music in the Virgin Islands is definitely Caribbean. You can hear reggae, steel pan, calypso and soca. Many other music venues can be enjoyed from Latin and blues to jazz and classical.

Virgin Islanders are religious people. Popular religions include Baptist and Catholic.

Superstitions and storytelling are very common. There are often stories about jumbies (spirits) that walk around in homes, on the street and anywhere the person telling the story wants them to be. Jumbie stories are a Caribbean tradition and are often used as cautionary tales for children. Bru Nansi, a spidery-man who prevails in the most adverse circumstance, is a popular story character.

In the Virgin Islands saying Good Morning, Good Afternoon and Good Night are not the same thing as saying Hello or Hi; the former is a warmer greeting and is the norm for friends and strangers.

While visiting the islands take your time to appreciate the local arts, events and music. Definitely try some local food, deserts and drinks, you will enjoy them. Make your vacation a true Caribbean experience by enjoying the local culture!

Island Terms: Mocko Jumbies: Colorfully costumed stilt dancers, They can be seen at carnival parades and other local events. The word jumbie refers to ghost-like spirits of West African belief.

Quelbe: Is a style of music and dance. The musical sounds that are danced to are made by scratching instruments made of hollowed out gourds. The band is called a scratch band.

Kenips: Are a type of fruit. They have a green outer shell and a fleshy edible meat around a large seed inside.

From Quelbé to calypso, it would be difficult to stroll along a street in the U.S. Virgin Islands and not hear music of some kind. Though quite diverse, the music of the U.S. Virgin Islands is a source of great pleasure and pride among islanders, whose rich history and cultural traditions are intertwined in myriad melodies and lyrics.

Quelbé, St. Croix's indigenous folk music, is an exuberant expression of Crucian life. Also known as "scratch band music," Quelbé musicians use hand-made instruments to create music of stunning originality that resonates with the history of the island. Quelbé instruments are varied, ranging from gourds and tin cans, to cane, string and wood – virtually anything that can be "scratched up." Historical events, everyday news and island life all are sources of lyrical inspiration. For those who appreciate native music and the significance of an oral history passed down through generations, Quelbé is an essential part of any visit to the islands.

Interestingly, scratch music dates back to the 18th century when the islands were under Danish rule. It was brought to St. Croix by West African slaves who worked the island's sugar plantations. The slaves' rich musical and story-telling traditions proved an enduring legacy. Influenced by the European colonists' own forms of music, the slave bands devised instruments using whatever materials they could find. These slave bands were the forerunners to today's scratch bands.

Quelbé, the official music of the territory, is most often heard at traditional and cultural festivals on St. Croix; but, along with steel pans, calypso and reggae, it can also be heard at night clubs, on the beach and in virtually any informal setting, as well as on St. John and St. Thomas.

Like Quelbé, calypso dates back to the arrival of the first slaves from West Africa. Banned from speaking to each other, the slaves began to communicate through song, using calypso. Today, calypso is heard most prevalently during Carnival, its lyrics often an amusing social commentary.

Equally captivating to visitors is quadrille, the traditional folk dance of the Virgin Islands. Quadrille originated in France in the 18th century as a court dance for Napoleon and first appeared in the Virgin Islands in the early 19th century. The quadrille dance varies from island to island; for example, on St. Thomas, the French German Quadrille is considered stately while, on St. Croix, the Imperial Quadrille is known for its amusing and animated style. Preserving and teaching the islands' unique folk dancing is the work of St. Croix's Heritage Dancers, a performing ensemble that can be seen regularly around the island.

Travel and Tourism

Travel Guide

In 1917, the US Virgin Islands officially became United States territories, 50 years after their previous owner, Denmark, first offered to sell the islands to the United States in 1867. Today, the US Virgin Islands have become the top destination for United States citizens wanting an exotic Caribbean vacation getaway without needing a passport.

The largest, most famous, and most frequently visited of the over 80 US Virgin Islands are St John, St Thomas, and St Croix. St Croix is situated several miles south of St Thomas and St John. Sixty percent of St John landmass belongs to the Virgin Islands National Park, which includes the desert Ram Head and forested Reef Bay trails. St John is also surrounded by the constantly changing Virgin Islands Coral Reef National Monument. St John Trunk Bay Beach, most famous for its underwater snorkeling trail, and Turtle Beach on tiny Buck Island are consistently ranked among the world most beautiful beaches.

The St Thomas capital of Charlotte Amalie contains the liveliest nightlife, finest restaurants, and largest collection of duty-free shops in the US Virgin Islands. St Croix Salt River Bay and historic capital of Christiansted are the only known sights Christopher

Columbus saw on current United States territory during his 1493 New World voyages. Although many US Virgin Islands visitors never venture away from the three main islands, tiny Bucks Island is worth a daytrip for its outstanding scuba diving, relaxing hiking trails, and breathtakingly beautiful Turtle Beach.

Most St Croix hotels are either modern North Shore beach resorts or picturesque Christiansted waterfront inns. Most St Thomas accommodations are situated in either Charlotte Amalie or the East End many beaches. St John contains a more limited, but more intimate, number of hotel rooms. Many former sugar plantations have been converted into self-catering condo complexes. Accommodation prices on all three major US Virgin Islands plummet between 25 and 50 percent during the low summer rainy season.

St Thomas Cyril E King Airport and St Croix Henry E Rohlsen Airport are the two main US Virgin Islands air gateways. There is no airport on St John, which can only be reached by boat. Ferries, cruise ships, and sailboats are also the most popular ways to travel between not only the three main US Virgin Islands, but also smaller islands such as Bucks Island and Water Island. Puerto Rico and the British Virgin Islands are also easy to reach by US Virgin Islands ferries.

Visitors not intimidated by driving on the left side of the road behind steering wheels placed on the left side of vehicles can easily rent cars on all three main US Virgin Islands. Large taxi buses, many of which are open air safari vehicles where up to 25 passengers are transported on open truck beds, are the most popular public land transportation throughout the US Virgin Islands. The smaller Water and Bucks islands can be easily explored by foot or bicycle.

High spot

    a) Charter a bareboat or fully crewed private sailboat to navigate the Sir Francis Drake Channel

b) Attempt to catch a giant blue marlin and add to the 20 world sports fishing records set on the US Virgin Islands during the last 25 years

c) Explore Trunk Bay Beach legendary underwater snorkeling trail

d) Cook over an open flame and reliving 17th century Danish West Indies sugar plantation life near the ruins of Annaberg

e) Take the Atlantic Ocean deepest scuba diving plunge beneath the Virgin Islands Coral Reef National Monument

f) Follow Christopher Columbus footsteps at the Christiansted National Historic Site and Salt River Bay

g) Take advantage of the Caribbean most generous duty-free limits and deepest discounts at the shops housed within former pirate warehouses along Charlotte Amalie Dronningens Gade

h) Soar above Charlotte Amalie skies aboard the St Thomas Skyride

Travel Tips

When traveling to the U.S. Virgin Islands, U.S. citizens enjoy all the conveniences of domestic travel including on-line check-in making travel to the U.S. Virgin Islands easier than ever. As a United States Territory, travel to the U.S. Virgin Islands does not require a passport from U.S. citizens arriving from Puerto Rico or the U.S. mainland. Entry requirements for non-U.S. citizens are the same as for entering the United States from any foreign destination. Upon departure, a passport is required for all but U.S. citizens.

Language: English may be the US Virgin Islands official language, but over a quarter of the islands population speaks other languages.

Spanish, spoken by nearly 17 percent of the US Virgin Islands population, is the most commonly heard language other than English. Many immigrants from French speaking Caribbean islands also speak French Creole.

Currency: The United States dollar, not surprisingly, is the official US Virgin Islands currency. For the most part, United States residents can withdraw funds from ATMs, spend their dollars, and use their major credit cards just as freely in the US Virgin Islands as they would back home. However, some smaller hotels and shops accept only cash payments. Travelers checks in United States dollars are also commonly accepted in most establishments. Currency exchanges are easy to find for visitors from countries outside the United States, whose currencies arent as commonly accepted as the United States dollar.

Time: The Atlantic Time Zone containing the US Virgin Islands is usually an hour ahead of Eastern Standard Time and four hours behind GMT (GMT -4). However, it is the same time in the Virgin Islands and the eastern United States during Daylight Savings Time, which the US Virgin Islands does not observe.

Electricity: The US Virgin Islands use the same 110-120V electricity settings and Type B plug sockets as the United States and most other parts of North America. Visitors from other parts of the world who need download converters should bring their own as they are hard to find on the islands.

Communications: The US Virgin Islands dialing code is +1, while the area code is 340. Cell phone reception can easily be found throughout the islands, whose main telecom network is AT & T Wireless GSM. Internet access is also widely available in the US Virgin Islands, and most major resorts contain Internet cafe.

Duty-free: No other Caribbean island boasts higher duty-free allowances than the US Virgin Islands. All United States citizens can bring back up to US$1,600 worth of merchandise, while those 21 years or older can also bring back up to 1,000 individual cigarettes or five cigarette cartons or 100 non-Cuban cigars. An additional liter of liquor produced in the US Virgin Islands can be added to the regular liquor limit of four liters for United States visitors over 21.

Tourism

In the mid 1900s the Virgin Islands saw the dawn of new times, more prosperous times. Tourist seeking the the warmth, beauty and relaxation the USVI offers, vacationed in the islands. Hotels, restaurants and shops began popping up on beachfront properties and in main towns. With the rise in business and economy came a rise in the population as immigrants from neighboring islands flocked to the USVI to work. Today the population of the USVI is made up of people from all over the Caribbean. The islands entered the new millennium as one of the premiere destinations for tourist visiting the Caribbean

The U.S. Virgin Islands is a paradise with so much more to offer than the traditional beach vacation. Visitors wishing to immerse themselves in a profound cultural experience can enjoy historical tours, culinary encounters, artisan fairs, parades, storytelling and other special presentations.

Walking tours on St. Thomas and St. Croix feature the diverse architecture, evidence of nations that colonized the islands in the 17th and 18th centuries. If you're feeling energetic, walk one of the many street steps, the most famous being the 99 steps on St. Thomas, a common way of getting to higher ground.

Your cultural journey continues with a look at the life and creations of artisans and crafters who earned a living creating functional and decorative pieces. Restored greathouses now serving as museums, like Haagenson House on St. Thomas and Whim Museum on St. Croix, preserve this past, displaying masterfully created mahogany pieces, delicate linens and original art. Local craft cooperatives, art galleries and artist colonies present the works of today's tradition-bearers. Annaberg Plantation ruins in St. John's National Park offers daily cultural demonstrations, including cooking the old-fashioned way – on a coal pot over an open flame.

In 2003, the Legislature passed a bill proclaiming "Quelbe, the vocal and instrumental style of the Virgin Islands' folk music which traces its ancestry to Africa and Europe. Quelbe is a fusion of bamboula rhythms and chants, cariso songs and melodies, and the official traditional music of the Virgin Islands."

Historically speaking, the scratch band sound that is Quelbe was created by slaves, self-taught musicians who made their own instruments and who lived and worked on sugar plantations. Since strict Danish laws forbade drum beating and dancing, slaves incorporated European sounds and dance steps into their practices. The newly created rhythmic styles produced "persuasion bands" that used homemade bamboo flutes, bass drums, steel triangles and squash (a dried gourd, grooved and scraped with a wire prong) to produce the sound. As they evolved musically and instrumentally, a new kind of music was born. Instruments changed through the years, including the addition of a guitar, tambourine, the "pipe" (an old tail pipe) which replaced the bass drum and the ukulele. The music offers commentary on such things as current events, cheating spouses and rum smuggling in ladies pantaloons. Modern-day Quelbe or scratch bands have an additional instrument or two and enjoy more popularity today.

Since African dance was also prohibited by plantation owners, slaves copied and adopted the Europeans' quadrilles, lancers, jigs, mazurkas, schottisches and other dances, giving them their own interpretation. The popular French quadrille was loved because of its hip swaying and rhythmic steps. Today's dancers wear madras costumes and handmade head ties. Groups like the St. Croix Heritage Dancers, who dance the French form of quadrille, perform with local Quelbe bands at special events and dances.

[Looking for a really unique adventure? Then you will love our Night Kayak Adventure with Pirate and Ghost Stories. From Blackbeard, Bluebeard, and Teach, prepare for an experience with a dash of history, a pinch of the macabre, and a spooky twist when you kayak along the dark and winding waterways of the Mangrove Lagoon. Enjoy the starlit sky as you look for stingrays, tarpon, and other marine life illuminated with lights below your kayak. You will go back in time and relive those days when pirates, ghosts, and jumbies still roamed the islands. Hear tales of shipwrecks and the eerie legends that haunt the islands to this day.]

National Park

In 1956 Laurance Rockefeller gave the National Park Service a generous gift of 5,000 acres of land on St. John. This gift along with subsequent additions have increased the holdings. Today almost two thirds of St. John's beautiful forest, shorelines and underwater lands are protected by the Park. Historical and marine treasures on St. Croix including Buck Island are also protected by the Park Service, as are portions of Hassell Island.

Water Island: The 4th Virgin Island

In 1996 Water Island, located in St. Thomas' Charlotte Amalie harbor, was officially returned to the USVI from the Department of the Interior. Today Water Island is the fourth United States Virgin Island.

Caribbean Culture: Have you seen a mocko jumbie? Heard the sweet sound of steel pan? Swayed your hips to quelbe or soca? Tasted kalaloo? Sample the islands' culture by trying island dishes, seeking out live music performances and attending cultural events.

Genealogy: Genealogy libraries are available on St. Croix and St. Thomas. They focus on records for the Virgin Islands and Caribbean region. Old books, maps, photos are also part of the collections. If you are interested in history it's worth a visit; and definitely if you want to conduct genealogy research.

Heritage Attractions: The islands of the USVI were a Danish colony until 1917. Learn about Caribbean colonization by visiting some of the historic forts, churches and homes located in the main towns. Plantation ruins on St. Croix and St. John can be visited.

Museums: Museums on St. Croix, St. Thomas and St. John house collections of West Indian Mahogany furniture, clothing, photos, artifacts from Amerindian inhabitation of the islands, plantation history, slavery, as well as items from modern times. Heritage museums also exist.

Photography: Stunning turquoise water, white sand beaches, brightly painted homes, tropical fruit stands, sunsets, sailboats... these are just some of the wonderful possibilities you can look forward to capturing. On island photographers sometimes offer specialty classes; like underwater.

Carnival

It's the biggest party of the year, and each island has its own. St. Croix's Christmas Festival starts in December with an adult's parade on Three Kings Day. St. Thomas's carnival culminates in the final week of April. St. John's celebration is Fourth of July week.

The first carnival was staged in 1912 during the final years of Danish occupation and lapsed during World War I. Revived in 1952, carnival has become the second largest festival in the Caribbean. A month-long series of dazzling pageants and talent shows is held to choose royalty to rein over the festival. Fun events such as a boat race, Greased Pig Contest and Toddlers Derby entertain everyone at the festivities. A series of elimination contests to crown top performers are called Calypso Tents. Calypsonions offer satirical commentary on the state of the islands, oftentimes mocking the shenanigans of politicians. Other popular events held during Carnival is j'ouvert, a morning jump up, a food fair presenting the islands' best traditional eats and a competition to crown the King and Queen of the parade troupes. A children's and adult's parade close the lively month with brilliantly costumed and decorated troupes and floats.

Virgin Islands National Park encompasses over half the island of St. John and almost all of Hassel Island preserving stories of the prehistoric past and over a hundred historic sites that together complete one the most undisturbed and comprehensive Caribbean landscapes.

Significant prehistoric sites are present on almost every beach and in every bay within the park. These archeological sites date from as early as 840 BC to the arrival of Columbus. There are early nomadic hunter-gatherer Archaic Period sites, followed by early chiefdom villages, then complex ceremonial sites and each with their own burial grounds. These sites have given us a greater understanding of this Caribbean region's prehistory, and the religious and social development of the Taino culture that greeted Columbus. These sites have dramatically increased our understanding of the ancient rock art that is found throughout the Caribbean islands. We now known when Caribbean rock art was carved, why they were carved in these specific areas, such as those found in the park at Reef Bay, their purpose, religious meaning and how they reflect cultural development.

After Columbus' arrival, the Virgin Islands' became one of the first melting pots, made up of many cultures from around the world. European powers competed for strategic and economic control. They brought enslaved workers from Africa. Historic landscapes and architectural remains of hundreds structures from plantation estates are found throughout the park. Ruins include windmills, animal mills, factories, great houses, terrace walls, and warehouses. In addition to these plantations are at least two thousand house sites that were occupied by the enslaved workers and their graveyards.

Restautants

Restaurants in the Virgin Islands range in style from roadside stands and beach bars to posh dining spots overlooking the sea.

Although each restaurant has its own personal style and ambiance, most restaurants in the Virgin Islands are consistently casual. In more elegant and formal dining spots, men should always wear a button-up shirt and slacks, and women should consider dressing in business casual. Skirts and dresses are never considered too formal. Less formal dining spots allow shorts and T-shirts, but bathing suits are rarely considered acceptable attire.

The culinary styles of the Virgin Islands is influenced by a wide array of flavors from many countries around the world, including France, China, Japan, Italy, Mexico, and other islands in the Caribbean. This means that no matter which island you are on, chances are you'll find something to fill every craving you experience. Because of the obviously easy accessibility to the sea, you will find that most restaurants serve up sea food in abundance. Okra is another island staple, and many visitors will find that the soups here are a departure from what they are used to - sweet instead of hearty, and often made up of fruits instead of vegetables. Learn more about the island's food and the restaurants serving them in the following table.

Restaurants By Cuisine		
Cuisine	**Restaurants**	**Locations**
American	90 Restaurants	Sapphire Beach, Nazareth, Coki Point, the vicinity of St. Thomas and St. John, Water Island, Bellevue, Havensight, Epworth, St. Thomas, St. John, Frenchtown, the North Shore, St. Croix, Montpelier, downtown Charlotte Amalie, Caneel Bay, Hull Bay, downtown Cruz Bay, Carlton, Concordia, Marina Cay, Golden Rock, the vicinity of Charlotte Amalie, Christiansted, Coral Bay, Cruz Bay, Frederiksted, Red Hook, East End, Catadupa, Charlotte Amalie, downtown Christiansted
Asian	3 Restaurants	downtown Cruz Bay, Maroon Town
Asian Fusion	1 Restaurant	Cruz Bay
Cajun	3 Restaurants	Frederiksted, St. Croix, downtown Christiansted
Californian	1 Restaurant	downtown Cruz Bay
Caribbean	92 Restaurants	Nazareth, St. Croix, the vicinity of St. Thomas and St. John, Frederiksted Southeast, Water Island, Bellevue, Havensight, St. Thomas, St. John, Frenchtown, East End, Cane Bay, Barret, downtown Charlotte Amalie, Bolongo Bay, downtown Christiansted, downtown Cruz Bay, Concordia, Friis Bay, Gifft Hill, Beef Island, Cooper Island, Cruz Bay, Frederiksted, Red Hook, East End, Charlotte Amalie, Christiansted, Catadupa, Coral Bay
Chinese	10 Restaurants	the vicinity of St. Thomas and St. John, Anna's Retreat, Havensight, Golden Rock, Frenchtown, Epworth, Red Hook, downtown Charlotte Amalie

Restaurants By Cuisine		
Cuisine	**Restaurants**	**Locations**
Continental	5 Restaurants	Frederiksted, the North Shore, Frenchtown, downtown Christiansted
Creole	4 Restaurants	Frederiksted, downtown Cruz Bay, Coral Bay, Cruz Bay
European	4 Restaurants	Frederiksted, downtown Charlotte Amalie, Frenchtown
French	5 Restaurants	Frederiksted, downtown Cruz Bay, Frenchtown, downtown Christiansted
Fusion	2 Restaurants	East End, Bellevue
German	1 Restaurant	Frenchtown
Greek	2 Restaurants	St. Croix, Charlotte Amalie
Indian	3 Restaurants	Christiansted, Frenchtown
International	48 Restaurants	Morningstar Bay, St. Croix, Bellevue, Cotton Valley, St. Thomas, Frenchtown, East End, the North Shore, Cane Bay, Anna's Retreat, downtown Charlotte Amalie, Caneel Bay, downtown Cruz Bay, Belvedere, downtown Christiansted, Beef Island, Coral Bay, Cruz Bay, Frederiksted, Red Hook, Charlotte Amalie, Christiansted, Catadupa
Irish	1 Restaurant	downtown Cruz Bay
Italian	29 Restaurants	downtown Cruz Bay, St. Croix, Water Island, Sion Farm, Christiansted, St. Thomas, the vicinity of Charlotte Amalie, St. John, Frenchtown, Cruz Bay, Frederiksted, Red Hook, East End, downtown Charlotte Amalie
Jamaican	1 Restaurant	downtown Charlotte Amalie
Japanese	6 Restaurants	Havensight, the vicinity of Charlotte Amalie, Cruz Bay, Red Hook, Maroon Town, downtown Christiansted

Restaurants By Cuisine		
Cuisine	**Restaurants**	**Locations**
Latin American	7 Restaurants	Charlotte Amalie, Frederiksted Southeast, Bellevue, Coral Bay, Frederiksted, St. Croix
Mediterranean	5 Restaurants	St. Croix, downtown Cruz Bay, Catadupa, Frenchtown, Charlotte Amalie
Mexican	11 Restaurants	downtown Cruz Bay, St. Croix, the vicinity of St. Thomas and St. John, St. Thomas, Christiansted, Cruz Bay, Red Hook, the North Shore, downtown Charlotte Amalie, downtown Christiansted
Pan Asian / Pacific Rim	4 Restaurants	downtown Cruz Bay, Bellevue, Cruz Bay, St. Croix
Scandinavian	1 Restaurant	Sion Farm
Spanish	2 Restaurants	downtown Charlotte Amalie, St. Croix
Tex-Mex	5 Restaurants	Belvedere, Christiansted, downtown Charlotte Amalie, St. Croix, downtown Cruz Bay
Thai	4 Restaurants	Red Hook, Christiansted, Frenchtown, downtown Christiansted
Vietnamese	1 Restaurant	downtown Cruz Bay
Contemporary	8 Restaurants	downtown Cruz Bay, St. Thomas, downtown Charlotte Amalie, St. Croix, Caneel Bay
Eclectic	13 Restaurants	Frenchtown, Charlotte Amalie, St. Croix, St. Thomas, Christiansted, Coral Bay, Cruz Bay, Frederiksted, Catadupa, downtown Charlotte Amalie, downtown Christiansted
Soul food	1 Restaurant	Coral Bay
Vegan	2 Restaurants	Frenchtown
Vegetarian	6 Restaurants	Frenchtown, downtown Charlotte Amalie, Coral Bay, the vicinity of St. Thomas and St. John, Charlotte Amalie

If you are still trying to decide where to stay, knowing more about the restaurants located at, or near, each hotel can sometimes be useful in the decision-making process.   You can learn about restaurants at specific hotels in several ways. First, consider visiting our article listing the Best Hotels for Dining Options. Or, select hotels that interest you from our extensive list (A to Z: Hotels in Detail), and read about their restaurants, as well as other nearby dining options within our detailed discussion of each property.

In the U.S. Virgin Islands, gratuities between 10 and 20 percent are typical, but the tip should reflect the quality of service you experience.

Vacationers looking for world class dining will be pleasantly surprised by Virgin Island fare. The region's restaurants cater to all types of visitors, from those interested in a casual bite to gourmands in search of a new taste experience.

Cousin

Visit one of our local restaurants where recipes are handed down through generations. Some of our favorites include pumpkin fritters, kallaloo (relative of gumbo), potato stuffing (try it for Thanksgiving) and, for a truly different dessert, red grout (a tapioca dish introduced by the Danes).

Pumpkin Fritters
1 ½ cups mashed pumpkin
¼ cup sugar
¼ teaspoon salt
1 teaspoon vanilla essence
1 teaspoon baking powder
1 ¼ cup milk

1 cup all-purpose flour

Oil for deep frying

Remove seeds and stringy fibers from center of pumpkin. Cut the pumpkin to smaller pieces for quicker boiling. Place in a pot and cover with water. Boil until pumpkin is fork tender. Drain water and scoop out pumpkin from outer shell. Mash with a fork. In a mixing bowl, combine pumpkin, sugar, salt, vanilla, baking powder, milk and flour and stir until ingredients are combined. An electric mixer is not recommended. Drop by the teaspoonfuls into hot oil and fry 1 to 2 minutes on each side. Drain on paper towels. Makes 12 fritters. Per fritter: 115 calories, 6 grams fat, 3 milligrams cholesterol and 86 milligrams sodium.

Kallaloo

"Kallaloo is for good luck in the New year, especially for lovers", said Arona Peterson, local food expert and author of Food and Folklore of the Virgin Islands. "The old folks believed that if you served kallaloo to your loved one on Old Year's night, there would be a wedding by June."

½ pound salted meat—pigtail or salt beef

Water

Ham bone if available; a common substitute is smoked turkey

1 (10 ox.) package frozen cut okra

½ large onion

Seasoning (thyme, celery, parsley—about 1 teaspoon each)

1 cup boned fish (a white fish with skin is preferable), fried

1 clove garlic

½ hot pepper (scotch bonnet works well)

1 (10 oz.) frozen chopped spinach

Soak salted meat in water for a few hours. As with the fritters, your world market may have pig tail. If it isn't salted, there is no need to soak it. Wash and cover with water. Bring to a boil. Lower heat and cook until tender. In the meantime, fry fish and allow to cool. Remove meat from water and set aside. Add water to half full level. Put in the ham bone or smoked turkey and okra. Add onions, seasoning, garlic, hot pepper, boned fish and spinach. Let simmer for an hour until mixture has stew consistency. Return meat to stew and simmer for another ½ hour. This stew is generally served with fungi, a cornmeal dish similar to polenta. I think a round or two of polenta would work just fine. Serves 8. Per one cup serving, 155 calories, 2 grams fat, 43 milligrams cholesterol and 307 milligrams sodium.

Potato Stuffing

This is such a favorite it's served with everything except fish. It makes a great surprise for your Thanksgiving dinner.

6 large white potatoes
4 tablespoons tomato paste
1 small onion, minced
¼ cup sugar
2 stalks celery
1 medium green bell pepper, minced
1 teaspoon hot pepper, minced
¾ cup vegetable oil
1/3 cup raisins
3 sprigs parsley
1 tablespoon salt
2 teaspoons thyme, chopped

Peel and cut potatoes and boil in salted water. When tender, drain water and mash. Add cooking oil to a pan and sauté raisins, onion, green pepper and celery until translucent. Add pepper and sugar. Pour this mixture, in batches, into mashed potatoes. Some oil may remain which can be discarded. Spoon stuffing into a greased baking pan and bake in 350-degree oven for about 25 minutes.

Red Grout (Rodgrod)

There's no doubt it was inherited from the Danes. Locally, it was traditionally served on Transfer Day (March 31). We enjoy the dish whenever we have a taste for it.

2 pints guavas with skins and seeds
¼ teaspoon salt
¼ cup quick cooking tapioca
2 cups water
1 cup sugar
1 teaspoon vanilla essence
Dash of mace
Dash of nutmeg
Dash of cinnamon

Wash fruit. Peel and cut up guava. Place in pan with 1 1/2 cups water. Simmer covered for 20 minutes. Strain. Save shells for later use. Measure liquid, adding enough water to make 2 ½ cups of liquid. Add sugar, salt and bring to a boil. Stir constantly. Mix tapioca in ½ cup of water and add slowly along with spices. Bring to a boil once more, stirring constantly. Remove from the heat when tapioca grains are clear. Add vanilla essence. Pour into a ceramic container or individual ramekins. Serve with heavy cream.

Things to Do in US Virgin Islands

Things to Do

Although visitors can easily explore even the largest of the 80 small US Virgin Islands on their own, a handful of reputable guided tours are readily available to those who want them. However, some guided tours are cancelled if not enough people join during the low summer season. Visitors can take US Virgin Islands tours by boat, jeep, air, or all of the above.

Most US Virgin Islands things to do involve sea, sand, and sun, but visitors looking for pursuits more active than sunbathing can cycle around Water Island, hike past numerous former plantation sites along St John Annaberg Historic Trail, or organize a private sailing excursion across the Sir Francis Drake Channel to the neighboring British Virgin Islands. Buck Island is St Croix most popular snorkeling and scuba diving site.

Sailing lessons are a must before navigating the several secluded inlets and coves around the US Virgin Islands beautiful, yet challenging, waters. *Jones Maritime Sailing School*, one of St Croix most reputable sailing schools, offers two-day weekend sailing classes aboard one of three 24-foot day sailboats. More experienced sailors can hire bareboat charters, without captain or crew, to travel across the Sir Francis Drake Channel. Fully crewed charters are also available, complete with captain and cook, for those willing to pay a little more for the security of traveling with an experienced sailing crew.

The only US Virgin Islands outfitter combining **sea kayaking** excursions with camping is St John *Arawak Expeditions*. All sea kayaks this Cruz Bay-based outfitter provides are made of fiberglass, include foot controlled rudders, and can seat two people. All meals, kayaking gear, and camping equipment are included in this outfitter fee. Many other US Virgin Islands hotels and outfitters offer sea kayaking tours.

Caradonna Dive Adventures offers the greatest variety of **scuba diving** packages across the countless shipwrecks, underwater caves, and coral reefs beneath the US Virgin Islands turquoise waters. Buck Island, perhaps the finest scuba diving and snorkeling site on St Croix, is just a day sail away from Christiansted. However, experienced scuba divers may also enjoy exploring the caves and tunnels at the underwater wall along St Croix north shore. Salt River Canyon dramatic drop-off is 1,000 feet high.

The US Virgin Islands have been the site of over 20 world records in sports **fishing** during the past 25 years. The mega blue marlin may be the most famous fish swimming around the US Virgin Islands, but visitors can also try to catch sailfish, tuna, and several other fish aboard sport fishing charters like those *Gone Ketchin* offers from St Croix Salt River Marina. Mandahl Beach rocky shore is a popular St Thomas line fishing spot.

The **hiking** tours St Croix based *Ay Ay Eco Tours and Hikes* offers range from three to six hours. The half-day tour of the secluded coastline and forests around northeast St Croix is especially spectacular. The tiny Buck Island also contains a lot of beautiful scenery within its mile long and mile wide area. Fortunately, no poisonous snakes lurk around any US Virgin Islands hiking trails, but trekkers should keep their eyes peeled for the islands official flower, ginger Thomas, famous for its trumpet shape.

Freedom City Cycles offers both guided **cycling** tours of St Croix and bicycle rentals to cyclists preferring to explore the island at their own pace. Cyclists will encounter both paved and unpaved roads while pedaling through St Croix rainforests. *Water Island Adventures*, as its name suggests, specializes in guided cycling tours of Water Island, which begin with ferry rides from St Thomas.

Paul and Jill Equestrian Stables, based in St Croix, ranks among the highest rated **horseback riding** stables in both the US Virgin Islands and the entire Caribbean. These Sprat Hall Plantation stables welcome riders of all levels, including complete beginners, and both their horses and the trails they use are considered first-rate.

St Croix offers the finest **golfing** in the US Virgin Islands at *the Buccaneer* course at a hotel outside of Christiansted and the *Carambola Golf and Country Club*. *The Mahogany Run* is the most challenging golf course on St Thomas. See in more details below:

Yes, you've found all the fun stuff there is to do while on vacation in the Virgin Islands. Whether you want some heart pumping activity like zip lining, or something much quieter like bird watching; you can read about it in this section. Find information on boat trips to neighboring islands, ecotours, playing a game of golf, participating in road race or fishing tournament, renting a stand up paddle board, scuba diving, taking a yoga class or having a massage. There is so much to do.

Tours

Aerial Tour: Get a bird's eye view of St. Thomas, Water Island and maybe St. John! Aerial tours are available on St. Thomas by seaplane, airplane and helicopter. Aerial tours are a fantastic way to see the islands.

Eco-Tours: Explore the wonderful natural environment on an eco-tour. Kayak tours are offered on St. Croix, St. Thomas and St. John. Hiking trips are also offered. Popular locations include within National Parks and reserves.

Island Tours: Stunning views, historic ruins, scenic drives, scenery, beaches, and towns can be explored by doing an island tour. The most popular option is an island tour by taxi, but you can also rent a car and do it on your own.

Rent-a-Car: Visit more remote beaches, stay longer at spots you particularly enjoy, explore the scenic lookouts, stop for lunch or a drink – do a tour at your own pace. Car rentals are available on St. Croix, St. Thomas and St. John. Golf-carts can be rented on Water Island.

Nature & Wildlife

Bird Watching: There are over 160 species of resident and migratory birds in the U.S. Virgin Islands. The largest variety can be seen from November through February. Purchase a birding book and go out on your own; or join a tour. The Virgin Islands Audubon Society is based on St. John.

Dolphins & Whales: Whales, primarily humpback whales, come to the Caribbean in winter to mate and raise calves. EAST, an environmental group on St. Thomas offers educational whale watching boat trips in February and March. Someday charters offer trips as well. Dolphins can sometimes be seen at beaches or while boating. It's a gift to see dolphins or whales, rather than a guarantee.

Farms & Farmers Markets: Farm visits and stays are possible on St. Croix. Classes are sometimes offered. A few organic farms exists, some are open for visits. Stop by a farmer's market for fruits and veggies. There is an annual agriculture fair on St. Croix; and two on St. Thomas.

Gardens: Enjoy a stroll through native and exotic trees, bushes and flowers, tropical fruit trees and medicinal herbs. There are botanical gardens on St. Croix and St. Thomas.

Hiking: St. John is home to the Virgin Islands National Park and its 20+ hiking trails varying in length and difficulty. Pick up a hiking map and head out to explore. On St. Thomas there is one maintained hiking trail. On St. Croix there are a few. The St. Croix Environmental Association often organizes group hikes.

Horse Riding: On St. Croix, St. Thomas and St. John it is possible to go horseback riding along trails, roads, in the forest and sometimes along beaches.

National Parks: There are five national parks in the Virgin Islands: the Virgin Islands National Park on St. John and Hassel Island; the Virgin Islands Coral Reef National Monument off of St. John; the Buck Island Reef National Monument off of St. Croix; the Christiansted Historic Site and Salt River Bay National Historical Park and Ecological Preserve, both on St. Croix.

Stargazing: Watching the stars is great and relaxing fun. Download an astronomy app and easily locate constellations. There is low light pollution in the islands; this means great night sky watching. Meteor showers are a fantastic treat for stargazers.

Turtles: Hawksbill and green sea turtles can be seen while snorkeling and swimming at beaches in the Virgin Islands. There are boat trips in St. Thomas that specialized in going to bays frequented by turtles. On St. Croix the Sandy Point National Wildlife Refuge is closed part of the year to allow leatherbacks to nest. Educational nesting and hatching watches are offered

Water Activities

Beach Days: There are plenty of beautiful beaches. Look through the beach guide for each island for photos and information. A visit to the Virgin Islands must include a few days of falling into a beach chair, rocking in a hammock, or playing in the sand and water.

Boardsports: Fans of boardsports will be happy to know that they can enjoy windsurfing, kiteboarding, surfing, wakeboarding, skimboarding and stand up paddle boarding while on vacation in the Virgin Islands.

Fishing: The Virgin Islands offer some of the finest fishing grounds in the world and its home to challenging sport fish like marlin and tuna. Whether you are a novice or a seasoned fisher, you can enjoy fishing in the Virgin Islands. There are tournaments throughout the year on St. Croix and St. Thomas.

Jet Skis: Jet skis are available in single and double riders and are often rented out by the ½ hour. Availability is limited by regulations and there are restrictions on where they can be taken; jet ski operators will provide instructions and guidelines. Some offer guided tours.

Kayaking: Kayak rental are available at some resort beaches and beach parks. Kayak tours are available on St. Croix, St. Thomas and St. John. Enjoy a relaxing and healthy paddle off a beach, gliding from shore and within the bay.

Scuba Diving: There are more than 58 dive sites of different levels off the shores of the U.S. Virgin Islands. Dive operators can safely guide you to and around them. They can take you out for the first time, teach you to dive, get you certified and instruct you for higher levels of dive certification.

Snorkeling: The underwater world fascinates, delights and intrigues. It's a magical place where fish of many colors dart in and out of rocky out rocks, turtles and stingrays swim by, seafans sway in the current – and you can floats above it all and observe

Boating & Charters
Dinghy Rental: Rent a dinghy for a fun day of exploring on your own. You can beach hop or pick a few snorkeling spots to visit.

Dinghy rental operators will provide you with instructions, directions and advice on places to go.

Island Hopping: The Virgin Islands (USVI and BVI) are made up of more than 120 islands and cays. Each island has its own unique atmosphere. Ferry service, inter-island air travel, boat trips and multi-day charters are available. Visit: Island Hopping

Long Term Charters: Spend a few days and nights aboard a chartered sailboat, catamaran or yacht. Long term charters combine the atmosphere of a Caribbean cruise and the quality and service of an exclusive resort into an experience that is better than both! A fantastic way to explore the islands. Visit: Long Term Charters

Power-boating: St. Thomas and St. John Boat Rentals A day of boating is great fun and sure to be one of your vacation highlights. Boat charters and rentals are available for half or full day trips. Go snorkeling, visit neighboring islands and cays, stop at popular beach bars; it's all in a day on the water.

Sailing: St. Thomas and St. John Day Charters Sailing conditions are perfect in the islands; great wind, warm weather, turquoise seas and gorgeous scenery. There are numerous sailboats and catamarans available for charter. Enjoying the magnificent waters around the islands will be a vacation favorite.

Sailing Lessons: So you've always wanted to sail. Why not in the Virgin Islands? Sailing lessons are offered for a few days or stay aboard the sailboat for a week with real-time learning. Sailing lessons are available on St. John and on St. Thomas. Courses include different levels from basic to advance.

Sunset Sails: Boating and sailing trips for a few hours during sunset are available. Most include light appetizers and drinks

Sports

Bikes & Cycling: St. Croix has a healthy cycling community, shops rent bikes and bike tours are available. It is also home to an annual Half Ironman competition. Bike tours are also available on St. John and Water Island.

Golf: Play a round of golf on St. Thomas and St. Croix. There is one course on St. Thomas, Mahogany Run Golf Course and three on St. Croix: Carambola Golf Club, Buccaneer Golf Course and Reef Golf Course. Tournaments throughout the year attract resident and visiting golfers.

Horse Racing: One of the popular spectator sports in the islands is horse racing. Racing fans head to Clinton E. Phipps Race Track on St. Thomas and St. Croix's Randolph "Doc" James Race Track.

Tennis: Tennis courts are available at most large resorts on each island. Public courts are also available. Plan your visit during a tournament and watch or participate.

Running/Walking: The islands are mountainous and sidewalks are limited. There are however popular spots on each island for walking and running. Active running associations on St. Thomas and St. Croix hosts runs and races throughout the year.

Sailing: A very popular pastime and sport in the Virgin Islands, you can go out sailing for fun on a day charter; or plan your visit around one of the regattas. There are yacht clubs on St. Thomas and St. Croix.

Swimming: Swimmers can enjoy doing laps on beautiful beaches. Races on St. Croix and St. John allow visitors and residents to test their skill in the water.

Competitions & Races: If you'd like to plan your visit around a competition, tournament, race or regatta please contact the race committee's website for information on registration

Other Activities

Virgin Islands Shopping, Casino, Gaming: There are video slot machines in independent locations, primarily at bars and restaurants, on St. Thomas. The only casino in the U.S. Virgin Islands is on St. Croix.

Geocaching: Geocaching is a treasure hunt of sorts; follow clues, mostly latitude and longitude positions found on a website for geocaching to find a cache site. Usually it's a container with a few trinkets. Geocaching.com shows 52 caches in the U.S. Virgin Islands ranging from popular vista points to beaches.

Shopping: There are numerous jewelry stores, art galleries, souvenir shops, vendors, and shopping areas where you can spend a couple hours or a couple days buying everything for watches and necklaces to t-shirts and magnets.

Yoga: Yoga is popular in the Virgin Islands. Some resorts offer sessions, if yours does not you can attend a class or two at a yoga studio. There are special offerings like beach yoga, SUP yoga, hanging yoga and a few other variations.

Spas & Massage: Pamper yourself with a massage or salon visit. Several spas on island offer massages, body wraps, facials and an assortment of other services to help you pamper yourself while on island. Private masseuses are available too

Holidays and Festivals

Colorfully costumed dancers on stilts, called mocko jumbies, are prominently featured in many US Virgin Islands holidays, from one of the world liveliest Valentine Day celebrations to the traditional Caribbean Carnival festivities. Although each of the US Virgin Islands has its own vibrant Carnival celebrations, St John best combines the Caribbean most famous festival with the United States own Independence Day. The final parade day of St John Carnival just happens to fall on the Fourth of July.

The beauty of the U.S. Virgin Islands isn't the only thing that draws vacationers back time after time. Many people come each year specifically to attend an event or festival. Even if that isn't why you've chosen to visit the islands, you may want to find out if there will be any celebrations going on during your stay.

Attending an event or festival is a great way to experience local culture, by sampling regional fare, viewing handmade crafts, and listening to Caribbean music. In the Virgin Islands, there are three categories of events and festivals that are particularly common: cultural celebrations, music festivals, and sporting events.

Cultural Celebrations

a) Mardi Croix Parade: An annual street parade, which takes place in March, features marching bands and Mocko Jumbies (mythical African characters on stilts).

b) Carnival: One of the Caribbeans largest and most well known celebrations is Carnival. In St. Thomas it occurs sometime between April and May, and on St. John festivities happen in June or July. Featured are street parades, live music, dancing, various competitions, and lots of family fun.

c) Crucian Christmas Carnival: Throughout the month of December and into January, St. Croix celebrates Christmas

Carnival-style with a series of events that are fun for the whole family. These include parades, the Miss St. Croix competition, boat races, concerts, a culture night, Jouvert, a food and arts festival, and fireworks. The Carnival has been held for over 60 years and each has a different theme; for example, in 2014 they celebrated "A Majestic Scene for Crucian Carnival 2014-2015."

Music Festivals

a) Arts Alive Concerts: Concerts held throughout the year at Tillett Gardens. Performances are usually musical ensembles and classical performers.

b) St. John Blues Festival: Blues festival in March featuring regional artists at Coral Bay Ball Field. Tickets range from $25 to $45(USD).

c) March Music Series: The March Music Series is all about promoting arts in the schools. Students take on a different musical theme each year, studying music and attending lectures leading up to several public performances on St. Croix, St. John, and St. Thomas.

d) Love City Country Music Festival: This first annual festival is scheduled for May, 2015 on St. John.

Sporting Events

a) St. Croix International Regatta: Series of yacht races and parties held in the middle of February.

b) St. Thomas International Regatta: Yacht racers from around the world participate in the annual race hosted by the St. Thomas Yacht Club. The event takes place in March.

c) Beach to Beach Power Swim: In May, swimmers get the chance to participate in a race between beaches set in the protected waters of the Virgin Islands National Park around St. John. Participants can swim solo or as part of a three-person relay team and have three course options to choose from ranging from one to three and a half miles.

d) Bastille Day Kingfish Tournament: A charity fishing event that also includes cash and prizes for participants, this tournament turns into a beach party with live music after the fishing has taken place.

e) St. Thomas Open: Golfing event held at the Mahogany Run Golf Course in August.

f) Love City Triathalon: Held in August, the Love City Triatholon has three different categories for atheletes to participate in. The first is the basic triathalon which includes a half mile swim, 14 mile bike ride, and 4.15 mile run. The second is the SUP Triathalon, in which a stand up paddle boarding takes the place of the bike ride. Finally, the Aquathon allows competitors to participate solely in the swim and run portions.

Other Events and Festivals
Food and wine festival
Valentine Jump Up: The Valentines street festival featuring loud street music, arts and crafts booths, food, dancing, and fun.

a) Chili Cook-Off: Each March the United Way of St. Croix hosts a chili cook-off to benefit charity. Visitors from the surrounding islands attend the event to sample more than 10 types of chili, and enjoy live music.

b) St. Patrick's Day Celebration: March in the annual parade around Red Hook with music at Molly Molones and traditional irish pub fare served all day.

c) Taste of St. Croix: Food and wine festival held at the Divi Carina Bay Resort in April.

d) Arts Alive Springtime Arts and Crafts Festival: This arts and crafts festival focuses on screen printing, is held at Tillett Gardens in the end of April.

e) Reef Jam: A May festival typically held in Frederiksted on St. Croix to raise money and awareness in support of conservation of the coral reef system. There are numerous events throughout the day including live music and tons of good food to eat.

f) Arts Alive Summer Arts and Crafts Festival: The summer sister of the Arts Alive Springtime Arts and Crafts Festival, features arts, crafts, live entertainment, and food.

g) Lifestyle Festival: Fun events such as concerts and beach parties mix with important lectures and booths on health and safety. This takes place in July.

h) Arts Alive November Arts, Crafts, and Music Festival: The fall version of the Arts Alive Springtime Arts and Crafts Festival, has live music as an added bonus.

i) Reef Festival: The Coral World Ocean Park opens its doors once a year, offering free admission to the public in order to promote marine education. Interactive activities get adults and children involved in such fun as sandcastle building, swimming, and of course, relating to sea creatures. The event takes place in November.

British Virgin Islands
Cultural Celebrations
a) Emancipation Festival: Each August the British Virgin Islands celebrate its emancipation from slavery, which occurred in 1834. Festivities include boat races, live music, and the annual freedom march.

Music Festivals
a) BVI Music Festival: The BVI Music Festival takes place on Tortola at Cane Garden Bay Beach. The event lasts for three days, and features about five local and international Caribbean artists each night. Tickets cost $20(USD), or $50(USD) to purchase a three day pass.

Sporting Events
a) Sweethearts of the Caribbean and Classic Yacht Regatta: This annual February yacht race is based out of the West End Yacht Club on Tortola. An after party is hosted by the Jolly Roger Restaurant.

b) Dark and Stormy Regatta: This yacht race is hosted by the Jolly Roger Restaurant on Tortola, and by the Neptune's Trasure on Anegada each March.

c) Spanish Town Fisherman's Jamboree/Annual Wahoo Fishing Tournament: The Spanish Town Fisherman's Jamboree/Annual Wahoo Fishing Tournament is the British Virgin Island's top fishing event. Held at the end of March or beginning of April each year, this event also features great food and live music.

d) BVI Spring Regatta and Sailing Festival: On top of yacht races that run from Nanny Cay to the Bitter End Yacht Club, there are also fashion shows, live music, and street parties during the BVI Spring Regatta and Sailing Festival. This event takes place in March and April.

e) Foxy's Wooden Boat Regatta: The Wooden boat race takes place on Jost Van Dyke each May.

f) Highland Spring HIHO: Windsurfers, SUP surfers, and WETS trimaran sailors race between the British Virgin Islands each July.

Other Events and Festivals

a) Karl Merklein Art Show: Each January Karl Merklein's original art, plus the artwork of other local artists, is honored with an annual show case put on by the Sunny Caribbee Art Gallery on Tortola.

b) Caribbean Arts and Crafts Festival: Handmade crafts are on display and for sale each March in Trellis Bay, Virgin Gorda. A fashion show of locally made items is a well-attended part of the event.

c) Virgin Gorda Easter Festival: Easter weekend on Virgin Gorda is filled with activities that includle a calypso monarch competition parade, nightly entertainment, and queen show.

d) Bust Your Kite: Another Easter weekend event, though this one takes place on Tortola. Delta Petroleum hosts a kite flying event, where each child is given a kite as a gift, and allowed to spend the day flying it.

e) Restaurant Week: If you're visiting the islands in November, you're in for a treat. This week long event includes the Taste of BVI on both Tortola and Virgin Gorda that brings chefs from the island together in one venue to share their best dishes; the Visiting Cook Off Chef which pits local chefs against a celebrity chef to find out who will win the title; and the final event, the Barefoot Gourmet Soirée which is an elegant five-course dinner that benefits students looking for a career in the tourism industry.

f) Anegada Lobster Festival: In December of 2013, Anegada added a new event to the line up; the Anegada Lobster Festival. For between $10 and $12(USD) a plate, guests can enjoy local lobster specialties created by the chefs of local restaurants while they enjoy live entertainment. It takes place over two glorious lobster-filled days and involves a culinary tour of the island by safari, scooter, or rental car and brings guests to sample three different plates at each restaurant that is participating that year.

Valentine Day Jump Up: Although Christiansted hosts four lively Jump Up celebrations per year, none are more famous than the St Croix community annual Valentine Day extravaganza of arts, crafts, food, and mythical mocko jumbies dressed in colorful silks and stilts. The calls of outdoor vendors and the sounds of local musicians fill the air during this upbeat Valentine Day celebration.

St. Thomas International Rolex Regatta: The â€œCrown Jewel of the Caribbean,â€� as this prestigious race is called, takes place at the St Thomas Yacht Club each March. This yacht race, considered among the most competitive in the world, attracts sailors from throughout the Caribbean, Europe, and North America. Although the main race course is situated near Christmas Cove, there are also several side races. The Pilsbury Sound Race takes yachters around St John and St Thomas countless coves, while a challenging distance race occurs between Charlotte Amalie harbor and St Thomas East End.

Transfer Day: The US Virgin Islands may have been United States territories for nearly a century, but every March 31, the islands celebrate their Danish past during Transfer Day. Special excursions to former Danish forts, buildings, and ruins are organized and Danish products are sold from shops and vendors on the day the islands were transferred from Danish to American territories.

A Taste of St Croix: Foodies will undoubtedly enjoy this annual one-day April festival at St Croix only all-inclusive resort, the Divi Carina Bay All Inclusive Beach Resort and Casino. No fewer than 50 of the region most renowned restaurants serve their finest dishes during this celebration of St Croix finest culinary talent. French and Italian food is served alongside traditional Cajun, Creole, and Caribbean meals. All festival proceeds go towards the St Croix Foundation.

Mango Melee and Tropical Fruit Festival: St Croix continues its reputation as the unofficial culinary capital of the US Virgin Islands with this annual late June tribute to the island most famous tropical fruit at the St George Village Botanical Garden. Although the festival grew to include other fruits after Hurricane Lenny destroyed the 1999 mango crop, mangoes continue to be this festival main focus. Visitors can sample several of the more than 80 different mango varieties grown throughout St Croix in the forms of mango butter, beer, wine, and even sushi. The festival also features mango cooking and eating contests.

St John Festival and Independence Day: Calypso musicians, colorful mocko jumbies, and a lively parade are the main ways St John celebrates both the United States Independence Day and the last day of its month-long Carnival celebrations on the Fourth of July. This day also features the crowning of Ms St John and the carnival king as well as a fireworks display rivaling many in mainland United States cities.

U.S. Virgin Islands Open/Atlantic Blue Marlin Tournament: This eco-friendly fishing festival awards trophies not only to the fishers who catch the most blue marlin, but also to those who tag and release the greatest number of fish. Fishers from across the globe are invited to participate alongside some of the world greatest anglers. All proceeds from this prestigious event, held in St Thomas during the August weekend nearest to the full moon, go towards the Boy Scouts.

St Croix Blue Bay Jazz Festival: Fort Frederik Beach and the Caribbean Museum Center for the Arts are the main venues of this November jazz festival held in Frederiksted each November. Some of St Croix finest jazz musicians perform alongside musical legends such as Tito Puente, Jr and Pete Escovedo. Mocko jumbies, food vendors, and arts and crafts accompany these free musical performances.

Locations inside Virgin Islands
St. John

Attractions

National Park Sites & Ruins, St. John

Until 1917 St. John was part of the Danish West Indies. The small colonial island was developed like many of its neighboring Caribbean islands with a plantation economy. Divided into large plantation estates that cultivated sugarcane, the island was dotted with mills for processing the cane, great houses for housing the owner or overseer, and slave huts for housing the forced labor force. The ruins of these plantation enterprises tell the story of the New World. The most popular are Annaberg Plantation and Cinnamon Bay Plantation.

St. John: Eco-Tours & Park Adventures

The Virgin Islands National Park's beaches, coral reefs, historic ruins and hiking trails provide endless hours of exploration and enjoyment on St. John, as well as inspiration and opportunities for reflection. Visitors can enjoy a variety of activities on the land and in the water. Some visitors explore the park on their own, while others prefer a guided tour.

Eco-Tours

St. John is home to the Virgin Islands National Park which preserves about 3/4ths of the islands forest, it also includes thousands of acres of submerged lands and waters that contain a significant amount of coral reefs, shorelines and marine life. What better way to enjoy, understand and appreciate the rich natural and historical elements protected by the National Park than with expert guides to lead the way.

Every year Virgin Islands EcoTours receives Best of Awards such as: Kayak Tours, The Best EcoTour and Best Attraction by the readers of the VI Daily News. Kayak Hike & Snorkel Adventures are offered at three locations: St. Thomas Mangrove Lagoon; St. John Honeymoon Beach; and Historic Hassel Island. Professional guides lead ecological and historical tours where you kayak, hike and snorkel in one unforgettable adventure of fun and learning. VI EcoTours received the Certificate of Excellence by Trip Advisor. Wedding, corporate and private groups receive personalized service. Book online or call toll free.

Activities in the VI National Park, St. John

Virgin Islands National Park

The Virgin Islands National Park on St. John encompasses miles of lush forest, historic plantation ruins, pristine beaches and coral reefs teaming with marine life. Trails weave by scenic lookout points, many ending at the shoreline of a wonderful beach. Sun seekers will be delighted by the beaches on St. John, which are some of the most beautiful in the Caribbean. The park is well developed which makes exploring the historical sites, beaches and trails easy and rewarding. The top points of interest are Trunk Bay, Cinnamon Bay, Cinnamon Bay Plantation ruins and Annaberg Plantation. These are just four of the dozens of beautiful areas you can explore. You can enjoy the National Park by boat, camping, fishing, kayaking, hiking, scuba diving, snorkeling, swimming and bird watching!

Brief History of the Park

In 1956 Lawrence Rockefeller, through the non-profit organization Jackson Hole Inc., donated 5000 acres of land on St. John to the National Park Service. On August 2nd of the same year United States Congress passed legislation to establish the Virgin Islands National Park. The legislation stipulated that the Park's holdings on St. John could not exceed 9,485 acres. St. John contains a total of 12,500 acres. In 1962 the boundaries of the Virgin Islands National Park were expanded to include 5,650 acres of submerged lands and waters that contain a significant amount of coral reefs, shorelines and marine life.

In 2001 the Virgin Islands Coral Reef National Monument was established from 12,708 acres of federally owned submerged lands off the island of St. John. This area, administered by the National Park Service, protects coral reef and mangrove habitat crucial for the biological diversity of the entire Caribbean.

In 1978 a large portion of Hassel Island, a small island within St. Thomas' Charlotte Amalie Harbor, was donated to the Virgin Islands National Park.

Hassel Island

Hassel Island is 135 acres in size of which 122 acres are part of the Virgin Islands National Park. Once a peninsula connected to St. Thomas, the land mass was separated in 1860 by the Danish Government in order to facilitate better water and vessel circulation in the Charlotte Amalie harbor. There are four historical structures on the island now listed on the National Historic Places Registry. One of these structures is the remains of a British military garrison built during a brief British occupation of the former Danish West Indies (what is today the US Virgin Islands) in the 1800s. Another historical site is the Creque Marine Railway which dates back to the mid-1800s and is one of the oldest surviving examples of such a railway.

The Virgin Islands National Park's diverse beaches, coral reefs, historic ruins and hiking trails provide endless hours of exploration and enjoyment, as well as inspiration and opportunities for reflection. Visitors can enjoy a variety of activities on the land and in the water. Some visitors explore the park on their own, while others prefer a guided tour with a park sponsored program, a boat charter or by taxi.

Beaches: Beautiful beaches are definitely a large factor in the allure of the Virgin Islands National Park. White sand, crystal clear water, great snorkeling, sunny warm climate and the tranquility of St. John lends to an unforgettable experience. The most well-known of St. John's beaches is without a doubt Trunk Bay; voted most beautiful, most photographed and is just overall a great beach. Cinnamon Bay is another very popular beach as is Caneel Bay, Hawksnest, Honeymoon and Maho Bay just to name a few. There are many beach options. Visit the St. John Beach Guide to help you decide.

Snorkeling: The marine environment in the National Park's waters are incredible. Coral reefs, sea fans, small and large fish, rays, turtles are all there for you to behold and appreciate. Trunk Bay has a 225-yard, self-guiding snorkeling trail marked by underwater signs that identify coral and marine life. Other beach accessible snorkeling sites are available like Waterlemon Cay, Lameshur and Caneel Bay. Visit: St. John Snorkeling

Diving: The Virgin Islands ranks as one of the Caribbean's premier diving sites. Some major points of interest include Whistling Cay, Haulover Bay and Reef Bay. For the safety of yourself and others, scuba diving is not permitted off designated swim beaches. Dive operators on St. John are available to rent gear from, teach introductory dive classes, certify and take you out diving! Visit: St. John Snorkeling

Hiking: There are 22 unique nature trails in the National Park, you are bound to find several that appeal to you. You can find an enjoyable 30 minute stroll through shady trees or an invigorating full day hike through Danish plantation ruins, mysterious carvings and lush forest. Whichever you choose you will be taken away by the beauty of the Virgin Islands National Park! Descriptions of each trail are available, select the pages you would like to view from the table below.

Hiking Trails (Northside)		Hiking Trails (Southside)	
Lind Point Caneel Hill Caneel Hill Spur Water Catchments Turtle Point	Peace Hill Cinnamon Bay Francis Bay Annaberg School Annaberg Area	Leinster Bay Johnny Horn Brown Bay Reef Bay Petroglyph	Lameshur Bay Yawzi Point Bordeaux Mountain Salt Pond Bay Drunk Bay Ram Head
		Hiking Trails →	

Special National Park Tours and Demonstrations

Contact the Visitor Center at (340) 776-6201, ext. 238 to inquire and make reservations for the special National Park interpretative programs listed below:

Annaberg Cultural History Demonstration

Visit Annaberg Sugar Plantation ruins and learn about sugar production, the slave trade during the period of European economic expansion in the West Indies and what former slaves did to survive after emancipation. Witness bread-baking on a coal pot, basket weaving and subsistence gardening demonstrations. Activities begin at 10:00 am and end at 2:00 pm on Tuesdays and Wednesdays for basket weaving, Wednesdays thru Fridays for bread baking and Tuesdays thru Fridays for gardening.

Snorkel Trip

Tuesdays at 9:30 am. Snorkel over a coral reef and discover the Parks underwater treasures. The ranger will point out different coral formations, the organisms that live there and explain how they relate to each other. In addition, you will learn what the Park is doing to protect these valuable resources. Bring your mask, snorkel, fins and a t-shirt to prevent sunburn. Program is not for novice snorkelers. Meet at Trunk Bay's west lifeguard stand.

Water's Edge Walk

Sundays at 10:30 am. Where the land meets the sea you will find the shoreline, a place of constant environmental change. Many plants and animals depend on this complex zone for their survival. For example, ghost crabs inhabit the white sand beaches scavenging for food, and mangroves provide shelter and protection for juvenile fish and crustaceans. Join a ranger and learn more about the coastal plants and animals. Meet at the Leinster Bay trail head below the Annaberg ruins. Shoes for wading are recommended.

Evening Program

Mondays at 7:30 pm, Cinnamon Bay Campground Amphitheater. (Except in September when campgrounds are closed.) The Evening Programs, entitled "A Ranger's Choice", include slide shows, talks or demonstrations on different topics about the Park and the island of St. John. Program topics include the flora, fauna, history and culture.

Reef Bay Hike

Every Monday and Thursday, at 9:30 am; schedule is subject to change based on demand. Space is limited. The secrets of St. John's tropical forest, petroglyphs, and sugar mill ruins come alive on this three-mile hike. The hike is mostly downhill, but is not necessarily easy due to its length, steep rocky terrain, short but strenuous uphill sections, and the prevailing heat and humidity. In addition, there is the remote possibility that deteriorating sea conditions might require hiking back uphill to the trail head. Visitors with circulatory or joint/muscle problems, other medical conditions, or with small children, should carefully evaluate their ability to do this hike. This hike includes transportation: a shuttle ride to the trail head (cost $5.00) and a boat pick-up which returns hikers to the Visitor Center (cost $15.00). All hikers must meet at the Visitor Center by 9:30 am. Participants should bring lunch, 1 – 2 liters of water per person, any special medication (taken daily) and a swimsuit for a quick swim at the trails end. Wear good hiking shoes (no open-toed footwear or aqua socks) and cool comfortable clothing.

Boating

Renting a boat and beach hopping is a great experience. You can also charter a boat with captain for a day or a yacht for a week or more. There are rental boat operations on St. John that rent small boats and dinghies perfect for a day of beach hopping via the sea!

Daysail charters will show you some of the beautiful shorelines and snorkeling areas of the National Park and often include lunch and drinks, making for a perfect and relaxing day.

Bird Watching

Bird watchers will enjoy hiking around St. John and in particular the Francis Bay trail. The winter months are the optimum time for bird watching. There are some 160 bird species known to the islands, including parrots, hummingbirds, pelicans, ducks, egrets and more. Contact the National Park Visitor Center about bird watching trips that they might offer.

Fishing: Fishing in Park waters is open only to hand held rods. No fishing is allowed in Trunk Bay or in any beach swimming areas. Spear guns are prohibited. Please read USVI Recreational Fishing.

Camping: Camping on National Park lands on St. John is restricted to the Cinnamon Bay Campground. Accommodations include bare tent sites, sites with tent-covered platforms already set up and small cottages. No backcountry or beach camping is permitted within Virgin Islands National Park.

Archeological Research

The Virgin Islands National Park Archeological Lab is located at Cinnamon Bay. This lab is open to visitors, who may want to take a peak at recently discovered artifacts, learn more about the archeological history of the island or volunteer. For information on the archeological research at Cinnamon Bay visit the Friends of the VI National Park website.

For Kids Junior Ranger Program

To help protect the natural and cultural resources of St. John, you are welcomed to join the Junior Ranger program on St. John. Stop by the Visitor Center and pick up a Junior Ranger workbook. Workbook exercises include "interviews" with trees, word searches, games and a nature hike. At the end, you return to the Visitor Center and you are awarded with a Junior Ranger program certificate, "Smokey Bear" hat, Junior Ranger badge and pencil. This is a fun, educational activity for kids to do while visiting Virgin Islands National Park.

Scenic Drive or Tour

Several roads around St. John have roadside observation points or photo stops giving you panoramic views of Trunk Bay, Maho Bay, Caneel Bay, Coral Bay and others. Roads are well maintained but narrow and sometimes steep. Renting a car and exploring is lots of fun. For those that rather not rent a car taxi operators can show you around.

Parties, Weddings, Picnics

Special use permits are required for organized activities that include ten (10) or more people for events such as weddings, birthday parties, etc. Picnic pavilions and grills are available for all activities.

However you choose to explore the Virgin Islands National Park you will undoubtedly leave with unforgettable memories of St. John.

The Visitors' Center, in Cruz Bay, is the place to start your exploration of St. John. The exhibits presented will introduce you to the park's history, hiking trails, historical sites andlocal flora and fauna. Park rangers can help answer questions about trails and hikes. Brochures about the Park, maps and books are also available at the center. The center is open daily from 8 am to 4:30 pm

The Virgin Islands National Park on St. John offers an assortment of unique hiking trails. You can find an enjoyable 30 minute stroll through shady forest to an invigorating full day hike.

Guided Walking & Hiking Tours

Take a walking or hiking tour in the National Park with a professional and knowledgeable guide and learn about the islands history and ecology.

The National Park Service offers a guided hike of Reef Bay Trail. It is lead by a ranger and is a popular choice. It takes place every Monday and Thursday at 9:30 am. The schedule is subject to change based on demand. Enjoy learning about the secrets of St. John's tropical forest, petroglyphs and sugar mill ruins on this three-mile hike. Reservations are strongly recommended as space is limited. Contact the National Park Visitor's Center on St. John for more information.

You can explore the trails within the National Park on your own as well..

St. John offers rest, relaxation and an adequate amount of sporting activities. Plan the activities you would like to do most and have a great vacation!

St. John offers rest, relaxation and an adequate amount of sporting activities. Plan the activities you would like to do most and have a great vacation!

Activities

St. John: Island Tours

St. John is well known for its beautiful vistas, beaches, lush forests, National Park and historical ruins. How do you take it all in is up to you. The most popular option is an island tour by taxi. You can also rent a car and do a self-guided driving tour; or explore the main town on foot. Make the do-it-yourself tour easy by grabbing an activity and road map before heading out to explore

Complementing the rejuvenating natural elements of St. John, like the blissful warm temperatures and tranquil waters, are opportunities to pamper yourself and to treat your body and mind to the health benefits of the healing arts. Spas on St. John offer body wraps, facials, hydrotherapy, aromatherapy and more. Participate in private yoga classes. Feel renewed on your St. John vacation by adding a massage session to your plans. Private masseuses are available and will usually come out to your hotel or villa. While on vacation, slow down and relax.

St. John: Fishing

Anglers will have a terrific time testing their skill and trying their luck while fishing on vacation in St. John! Go offshore in pursuit of Marlin, Dolphin Fish (Mahi-Mahi), Wahoo and Tuna. Or try inshore fishing and see whether you can get some Kingfish, Barracuda, Jacks or Yellowtail Snapper to bite!

Wondering if your big catch, the one you will be talking about for years to come, will be in season at the time of year you are planning your visit to St. John. The quick answer is that some species are around all year and others have peak seasons. Experienced fishing charter operators and captains in the area know the islands' waters and seasons. They can provide information on what you might find on the end of your line when you go out fishing with them during your St. John vacation.

Fishing charters on St. John offer trips that will excite everyone from the seasoned pro to the novice. They include inshore, offshore and marlin trips. Most operators offer trips lasting: ½ day (4 hours, typically between 8am and noon, or 1pm and 5pm); ¾ of a day (6 hours); full day (8 hours); and Marlin trips (10 hours, usually 7:30am to dusk). Short trips are generally inshore fishing only. Boat capacity of 4 to 6 passengers is common. Rates for fishing charters varies depending on length of trip, size of boat, inclusion of fuel in the rate versus fuel being a surcharge, and differences in services and equipment provided. Fishing charters generally have the details of their trips listed on their websites, and can provide the information by email or telephone upon request. Explore your options; book a fishing trip and a have a great time

Are you looking forward to eating your catch? Guests can typically request some of their catch, for example up to 20 lbs, the remainder stays with the boat. If you are interested in keeping some of your catch to take back to your vacation villa to cook for dinner be sure to ask about it. If you are staying in a hotel, ask the captain for suggestions of restaurants on the island that will cook your catch for you!

If you are really a fishing enthusiast you might consider planning your vacation to St. John around a fishing tournament, to be a spectator or to participate! Some fishing charters are available for tournaments. You'll find various tournament options on neighboring St. Thomas, there aren't any hosted on St. John. Here is a sample: Couples Tournament (February), Dolphin Derby (April) and the USVI Open/Atlantic Blue Marlin Tournament (August).

St. John: Scuba Diving

The underwater world in the Virgin Islands is stunning and truly amazing! Explore corals and gorgonian forest of sea fans and sea whips. Dive around caves, explore sunken boat wrecks or take a night dive and explore the fantastic world of nocturnal marine life! Swim among turtles, bright parrotfish, blue tangs, schools of fry and so much more.

The marine environment around St. John is world class and there are world class dive operators here that can take you out for the first time, teach you to dive, get you certified and instruct you for higher levels of dive certification

Diving around St. John is best described as fantastic, safe, easy and fun. There are more than 25 dive sites within a fifteen minute boat ride. The diving consists of shallow coral gardens, shear rock faces, fringing coral reefs combined with an abundance of tropical fishes. Visibility ranges from 50-100 ft, and water temperature between 78-84 degrees. We offer 2 tank dives for certified diver's every morning of the year. In the afternoons, we offer intro to scuba, single tank dives and snorkel tours. Certification courses are available upon request.

The best conditions for diving in the islands are found during the summer and fall months, with visibility generally between 60 and 100 feet. Some sites, particularly in Pillsbury Sound, can be explored all year round as they are protected from the wind and rough seas that can affect other more open sites during the winter months. St. John and St. Thomas are close enough to each other that they share many of the same dive sites in the Pillsbury Sound area including Carval Rock, Congo Cay, Grass Cay, Mounds at Mingo, Arches and Tunnels of Thatch and Lovango Cay.

There are over a dozen dive sites around St. John. Most are shallow dives and many only 15 to 20 minutes away from the shore/dock. In addition to those located in the Pillsbury Sound other popular dive sites include Eagle Shoal, Flanagan Reef, Maple Leaf, Cocoloba and Witch's Hat.

Dive operators are familiar with the various dive locations and can safely guide you to and around them. An introductory course will run around $60 to $110. For the certified diver; two morning dives are around $95 and it is around $85 to $100 for a night dive. Certification course, $260-$400. Multi-day dive packages are also available. Whether you are a novice or a dive enthusiast, there is no better place to dive than in the warm, inviting waters around the Virgin Islands.

Scuba Diving Tips

1. There is an excellent recompression chamber in the Schneider Regional Medical Center on St. Thomas. It is on 24 hours a day.

2. Always check your equipment before each dive.

3. Never dive alone.

4. Enjoy the sites, but don't touch.

5. The survival of the under water world depends largely on us; do not overturn rocks, kick up sand, pick up animals, touch coral. Be content with watching.

6. Leave the underwater world as you found it; future divers and the marine life will be happy you did!

7. Do not scuba dive if you are pregnant, too little is known about the effects of pressure on fetal development. Ask your doctor and/or dive professional for more information.

St. John offers rest, relaxation and an adequate amount of sporting activities. Plan the activities you would like to do most and have a great vacation!

St. John: Powerboat Rentals & Charters

Rent a boat, power or sail, and plan your own itinerary; stop at a few snorkeling spots, have a nice picnic on a deserted beach or a fun family trip to a neighboring island. Boats include; 25-28' Makos, 25' Boston Whalers, 26' Prowler Catamarans, 24' Island Daysailers, among others. Rentals are usually equipped with iceboxes, so you can travel with food and drinks. Boat rental operators will advise you of good locations to visit and provide you with maps and directions. They prefer you have some experience with navigating a boat and some require knowledge of local waters. Captains are available if necessary for an extra fee, usually around $80 for ½ day and $115 for a full day. Prices range from around $280-$650 for ½ day rentals and $385-$700 for a full day, in addition to fuel consumed. Prices vary based on type and size of boat. Visit our featured boat rentals!

St. John Boat Rental

Home of the $99 gas guarantee with the most professional crew in the islands. Pick from a variety of private charters boats legally certified for up to 12 passengers. We have boats for every budget starting at $450. Call for details (813) 465-2665 or visit stboat.com.

Aqua Blue Charters

Aqua Blue Charters is owner-operated, so we can provide you personalized service for your best day of island hopping in the BVI and USVI. Create your itinerary with your private captain and tour guide before your trip. From snorkeling in St. John and the Indians, lunch at the Willy T or on Jost Van Dyke to sipping afternoon drinks at Soggy Dollar, the day is yours. We believe our expert knowledge of the best cruising area in the world will exceed all of your expectations. Our boat Mojo, comes with snorkeling gear, drinking water, ice, tons of shade and bean bag chairs to provide the most comfortable ride possible.

Take It Easy

What do Brad Pitt, Kenny Chesney, and Cate Blanchett all have in common? They have all cruised on Take it Easy! Explore the islands in luxury! The day is yours! Whether it's with family, friends, a wedding party, or private getaway; you will surely enjoy the crystal blue waters and the warm Caribbean sun on TAKE IT EASY. This luxurious 45' Sea Ray can accommodate up to 12 passengers in comfort and style. We pick up at the National Park Dock in Cruz Bay. Visit our Facebook page at www.facebook.com/pages/Take-It-Easy-VI or our website for more information. Check out our excellent reviews on Trip Advisor!

Island Roots Charters

Explore the islands both above and below the water aboard Island Roots, a 25' fuel efficient World Cat Power Catamaran with U.S. Coast Guard Licensed Captain and PADI Certified Dive Instructor, Jason Siska. Island Roots Charters specializes in snorkel trips and island hopping to the most popular and most secluded spots in the U.S. and British Virgin Islands. Born on St. John and having spent the better half of his life there, Captain Jason is knowledgeable of the marine life, natural history, and local tales of these islands. Let him show you an experience worth remembering as you explore this Caribbean paradise.

Elixir Charters

Elixir, a sixty foot custom Hatteras Motoryacht is the largest and finest day charter yacht in the Virgin Islands. Allow us to pamper you with an eggs benedict breakfast and filet mignon and lobster tail lunch served to you at a bronze sea turtle table on our shaded aft deck. Enjoy three fabulous snorkel/beachfront stops, top quality snorkel gear, double kayak, fast inflatable, double hammock, giant sun pad, air conditioned salon with Bose home theater system, and our open top shelf bar including vintage wine and champagne. Full day trips and sunset dinner cruises daily. BVI trips available on private charters. Unforgettable!

Ocean Runner USVI

Let us provide the best day of your vacation! Whether you want to visit the BVI, cruise around locally with or without a captain, or sail the beautiful Caribbean waters, we have what you need. Conveniently located right in Cruz Bay, we have the finest fleet of boat rentals available, as well as a team of knowledgeable captains ready to show you the best the islands have to offer. Each boat is equipped with a large cooler and Bluetooth speakers. Snorkel, GoPro, and fishing gear are available to personalize your experience! Learn more from our guests on Facebook, Instagram and Twitter!

Sonic Charters

Sonic Charters offers private custom day trips to the U.S. and British Virgin Islands on 32' Intrepid and 33' Jupiter center console power boats. Whether you want to party the day away or lay back and unwind, we want to make it happen! With comfortable seating for up to 9 and capacity up to 12, Sonic Charters can provide unsurpassed luxury for a fun filled day. The USVI and BVI are an open canvas to explore and our local captains can take you to places other companies won't! We look forward to spending the day with you!

Lion In Da Sun

Lion In Da Sun uses a 28ft Scout powerboat providing stability, speed, and open bow seating while island hopping on a day trip. Discover what the area is known for; snorkeling, beachside restaurants and bars and white sand beaches. Visit the BVI islands of Jost Van Dyke and Norman Island or head to the Baths for the day. Stay in U.S. waters and see all of what St. John has to offer in the bays and cays surrounding the island. Ultimately the entire trip is up to you; we are however more than pleased to help you design it and then boat you to the best day of your vacation!

Rockhoppin' Charters

Explore the USVI or BVIs on board of our comfortable 32 FS Regulator Powerboat with twin Yamaha 250s. It has cushioned, forward-facing seating and will provide a comfortable, dry ride. Join us on a day trip, half day trip or sunset cruise out of Cruz Bay, St. John. Our experienced Captains Steve and Tyler can take you anywhere in the USVI or BVI: Jost van Dyke, Norman Island, Willy T, Peter Island, Cooper Island, Tortola, Virgin Gorda, Anegada... and will make sure you have a great day on the water. We also offer paddle board rentals, check out our SUP division: SUP-stjohn.com.

Caribbean Blue Boat Charters

AFFORDABLE PRICING for Families & Friends! Rent a Private Boat w/Captain! Our Stylish 36ft Marlins provide a most comfortable ride. Feel the wind as you cruise the islands. Listen to Buffet, Reggae or your choice from our 12 speaker surround sound. Your Day, Your Way! Snorkel w/ turtles, rays & tropical fish. Explore around St. John, visit The Baths, Virgin Gorda, Jost Van Dyke, Willy T's or relax on a beautiful beach. Call us today to help design an unforgettable trip! All things are possible! Includes seating up to 12ppl, snorkel gear & bathroom. Our Captains are FUN & experienced. Visit TripAdvisor/Facebook. Call or Text, we book up fast!

Beach Bum Boat Rentals

Don't just "rent a boat"... have the best day of your vacation! We have the largest selection and widest variety of stylish and comfortable boats for rent on St Thomas & St John. Large group? We can accommodate up to 32 people on one boat! Swim with turtles, rays and dolphin, lay on white sand beaches, sip a Painkiller in a hammock at the Soggy Dollar Bar, and enjoy the spectacular beaches of the U.S. & British Virgin Islands. Your captain will customize the perfect day for you. Flexible cruise ship schedules. Reserve your day early, we book up fast!

Cruz Bay Watersports, "Island Time"

This yacht is professionally crewed and able to entertain weddings, private charters and groups to 70 passengers. Experience the "Limousine style" of comfort, speed and amenities aboard the 60 foot Express Cruiser, "Island Time". Two decks, sun and shade, two boarding ladders, two warm water showers, upholstered seating and stereo throughout make for a very comfortable day on the water. Three trips a week to the Baths and Caves. Available for half day, full day, sunset sails, weddings, and private charters. Island Time departs from Westin Resort St. John, and is available for inspection on request.

See and Ski Powerboat Rentals

See and Ski is the choice for chartering a boat by the St. Thomas/St. John community. The fleet features 26' Prowler Cats, powered by fuel efficient and reliable engines, equipped with full biminis for extensive shade coverage, coolers, ample dry storage and freshwater showers for your comfort. Known for their smooth, dry ride, the twin hulls take all sea conditions easily. Island Hop, Beach Bar it, Fish, Dive, Spearfish or Snorkel. Checkout is streamlined. Your itinerary is individual to make it your day! Best Captains in the VI - experienced, knowledgeable & FUN! Explore, play, see & ski, the beauty of the Virgin Islands!

One Love Charters

Experience the British Virgin Islands and the U.S. Virgin Islands the way the locals do! Book with One Love Charters and you'll be able to visit all the destinations the VI has to offer... Including the ones you can't read about! Whether you want to snorkel beautiful reefs, bar hop beach to beach, or just relax on the boat with an ice cold beverage in hand, One Love Charters will work to make your day with us the highlight of your vacation!

Magnum, V.I.

Voted "Best Powerboat Rental" and "Best Tour Guides" of the Virgin Islands on St. John 2015! Get ready to experience the best part of your vacation - a day on the water with Magnum V.I.! Sit back and relax on our custom 32' Ocean Pro and let our seasoned Captain take you on an adventure as you explore the plethora of world-class snorkeling sites and the numerous beach bars you'll find throughout the U.S. and British Virgin Islands! Give us a call or stop by our information booth conveniently located across from the Cruz Bay Post Office and next to Uncle Joe's BBQ on St. John.

St. John: Snorkeling & Snuba

Snorkeling

From new, never snorkeled before to seasoned snorkelers there is something for everyone. Rocky coast lines, near shore reefs, off shore cays and sunken items like ships and planes provide beautiful and varied snorkeling opportunities. The conditions are; great visibility, fairly constant water temperatures of 79-83 degrees year-round, calm seas with little current and fantastic underwater scenery. In other words, perfect for snorkeling. View gorgeous underwater gardens of coral and visit with the residents; turtles, rays, octopuses, moray eels and an abundance of fish large and small. With the use of a mask, snorkel and fins you can float on the surface and admire the marine life below. Snorkeling is an option from beaches and also by boat trips

Eco Hike & Snorkel Tour: Lind Point to Honeymoon

Explore the best of VI National Park above and below the water. Depart from the Visitor Center in Cruz Bay and hike the Lind Point Trail. Learn about flora, fauna, cultural and historical trivia along the way. At Honeymoon Beach your guide will teach you to snorkel and identify the colorful sea life. The final portion of your hike takes you through a grove of wild cinnamon, the botanical gardens of Caneel Bay Resort and the ruins of a Sugar Plantation. Perfect for wedding, corporate and private groups. Book online with Virgin Islands EcoTours or call toll free.

Caneel Bay Kayak, Hike & Snorkel Adventure

Listen to our guests! We are ranked #1 in Trip Advisor: "Best Experience on St. John", "Do it early in your trip", "Amazing Adventure", "Great family activity", "Learn and have fun exploring

St. John!", "Very interactive tour of the islands unique ecology with a great staff.", "Don't miss this!". Kayak on turquoise waters, hike along scenic Turtle Point Trail and snorkel over coral reefs and see colorful fish, turtles and sting rays. Consider upgrading to a 5 hour tour with lunch: The Best of Henley Cay and Caneel Bay! Limited availability, reserve early. Book online or call us toll free.

Honeymoon Beach All-Inclusive Watersports Daypass
Experience St John's most romantic beach with the All-Inclusive Day Pass that includes: snorkel gear, life jacket, lounge chair, pool float, kayak, standup paddle board and locker. Enjoy island time in a hammock! Snorkel with sea turtles! The Honeymoon Hut sells cold drinks and souvenirs with food available. Taxi to Caneel Bay and walk 8 minutes to Honeymoon Beach or hike the Lind Point Trail from Cruz Bay. Perfect for wedding, corporate and private groups. $49 per adult and $10 per child. Book online using promo code VINOW for 10% discount or call toll free.

Henley Cay Kayak & Snorkel Adventure
Henley Cay is one of St John's premier snorkeling spots! Kayakers and snorkelers love the challenge of a 20 minute paddle across Caneel Bay from Honeymoon Beach to Henley Cay, part of the VI National Park, a UNESCO Biosphere Reserve. The protected beach is fringed with colorful coral reefs teeming with schools of vibrant fish and marine life. Flocks of seabirds fly overhead and feed close-by. Consider upgrading to a 5 hour tour with lunch: The Best of Henley Cay and Caneel Bay! Perfect for wedding, corporate and private groups. Book online using promo code VINOW for 10% discount or call us toll free.

Best of Henley Cay and Caneel Bay Adventure
Enjoy the Best of Henley Cay and Caneel Bay Kayak, Hike & Snorkel Adventures "combined" into a 5 hour tour with a picnic lunch! Henley Cay is among St John's most colorful snorkeling destinations.

See coral gardens, schools of tropical fishes and marine life at this deserted island. Seabirds soar overhead and feed nearby. Explore the Caneel Bay Peninsula. Kayak turquoise waters, hike Turtle Point Trail and snorkel to see turtles and sting rays. Look for deer, wild donkeys, mongoose and hermit crabs. Departs daily from Virgin Islands EcoTours' Honeymoon Beach Hut. Book online or call toll free.

By Boat Charters
Charters for ½ or full day trips can take you out to two or three unique snorkeling locations within protected marine areas in the Virgin Islands National Park. Day charters often include lunch, drinks, snorkeling gear, a little history or stories by the captain and overall a combination of enjoying the weather, boating and snorkeling.

Fins, a mask and a snorkel
Some of the popular beaches have watersports booths that rent snorkel gear. You can also rent gear for a few days from a dive shop. A popular question by visitors is "Should I buy or rent a set". Frequent visitors agree that you should buy a set. Here's why. To enjoy snorkeling your gear needs to fit you well, particularly your mask. A leaky mask can ruin a snorkeling experience. When buying your mask test it out by holding it to your face without the strap behind your head and inhale slightly through your nose. Let go of the mask, it should say in place; this indicates a good seal. Your fins should fit you snugly when dry because when you get in the ocean the water acts as a lubricant. Snorkels are easier because they are mostly one size fits all. If you get a bag for your gear make sure its a mesh type bag so that water and sand can drain out. An underwater camera is a great accessory; you can pick up a disposable underwater camera at your local supermarket. Another neat

accessory is a Fish ID Card; a small, waterproof card that includes popular marine animals you might see while snorkeling.

Snuba

For those of you who like snorkeling and are not divers there is a middle ground option called super snorkeling! There are several types of super snorkeling, however only Snuba is available on St. John.

Snuba enables people with the use of a mask and breathing tube attached to a tank of air floating on the surface to explore shallow coral reefs and marine environments while swimming under the water. Available to anyone from eight years old and up and doesn't require experience.

St. John offers rest, relaxation and an adequate amount of sporting activities. Plan the activities you would like to do most and have a great vacation!

Tip: Don't snorkel alone. Don't touch or stand on coral, it is very fragile. Don't feed the marine life non-fish food. Cereal, cake, bread, nuts, dog biscuits, leftover hotdogs from lunch are not part of marine creature's natural diets and are considered unhealthy for them. Do wear sunscreen on your back or wear a t-shirt. You can easily spend 30 minutes to an hour floating along admiring the fish and that is plenty of time for the bright tropical sunshine to leave you with a painful sunburn.

St. John: Sailing Charters & Excursions

Going on a charter is often the highlight of vacations to St. John. Enjoy the wonderful weather, beautiful waters and the service of professional and knowledgeable captains and crew. Sail or motor into quiet coves, snorkel at beautiful reefs and just bask in the delightfully warm sun and tropical breezes. Or take a sunset sail and enjoy the tranquil beauty and romance of Caribbean evenings. Many charter boats are 6-packs, holding a maximum of 6 passengers. There are larger boats that can accommodate groups. Charters are available in ½ day trips, full day, sunset sails, dinner cruises and also overnight trips or Term Charters. Prices range from about $50 to $150 a person depending on charter and length of charter. Amenities vary but might include open bar, lunch, snorkel gear, floats and other water toys. Visit the featured charters below!

Goddess Athena

Join us for unique adventures aboard our stunning, one-of-a-kind pirate ship! Queen of the Fleet for over 40 years, her 84 feet of classic lines make Goddess Athena a sight to behold. Friendly, knowledgeable crew, wonderful food and drinks, and sailing/snorkeling excursions tailored to your tastes will provide memories to last a lifetime. We invite you to experience the magic of sailing as only the pirates of the Caribbean knew. Our record 100% guest satisfaction speaks volumes. Join us today aboard the Goddess! Cannons by Request. Busty Wenches by Appointment Only. Sailing from Cruz Bay, St John.

Cimarron Yacht Charters

One of the most beautiful sailing vessels available for charter in the Virgin Islands. Join Coast Guard Licensed Master Captain Rick Smith aboard his one-of-a-kind classic wooden yawl for the best day of your vacation. Snorkel hidden reefs, take the helm and sail, or relax and enjoy. Every trip is customized. At 43' Cimarron offers ample space to stretch out. Snorkel Gear and Open Bar is included on every trip. Offerings include half-day and full-day snorkel trips, Full-day Jost Van Dyke / Soggy Dollar Bar, Overnight trips and more. Cimarron can comfortably accommodate groups of up to 12. Book Today!

Cruz Bay Watersports, "Island Spirit"

This yacht is professionally crewed and able to entertain weddings, private charters and groups to 70 passengers. Experience the comfort and amenities aboard the 60 foot sailing catamaran "Island Spirit". The vessel is unique featuring a "water slide", large U shaped bar for beverage/food service, upholstered seating in sun and shaded areas, boarding ladders for beach landings, warm fresh water showers and stereo throughout the vessel. Three trips a week to Foxy's & Soggy Dollar Bar, half day snorkel sail & sunset sails. Available for half day, full day, sunset sails, weddings, and private charters. Island Spirit departs from Westin Resort St. John, and is available for inspection on request.

Scubadu

Scubadu is a 43 by 25 foot luxury Catamaran, specializing in private day, sunset, and/or dinner sailing excursions. Leave the crowds behind as you explore the beautiful waters, islands, and beaches of the U.S. Virgin Islands. We sail to beautiful snorkel and swimming spots you can't get to by car. Scubadu departs from Cruz Bay, St. John or Red Hook, St. Thomas. Because we only do private charters for a maximum of 12 people, we can customize your trip to your groups' needs. We provide the Captain, first mate, delicious food, beverages, snorkel gear, and fresh water showers. All you need to bring are towels and non-spray sunscreen.

Catania Yacht Charters

Come Sailing with Catania Yacht Charters: excursions in the USVI and BVI, specializing in small groups of up to 6 guests. Catania is a traditional 80 year old sloop with a legacy of spending over 30 years circumnavigating the globe. Be pampered on an unforgettable excursion of a lifetime. Captain Ocean will enthrall you with the history of the Virgin Islands and stories of his around the world voyage. Discover pristine white sand beaches and enchanting hidden coves. Experience an underwater world full of spectacular marine life. Enjoy refreshments from our open bar. Full day, half day, and sunset sails available.

St. John offers rest, relaxation and an adequate amount of sporting activities. Plan the activities you would like to do most and have a great vacation!

St. John: Watersports

The Virgin Islands has a huge playground all around its islands; the ocean! Our beautiful ocean and beaches combined with gorgeous year-round summer weather make Watersports hugely popular for residents and visitors. Whether you are looking for a bit of high in the sky fun with parasailing or a bit of speed with waverunners, you'll find them on St. John. If you have a sense of adventure, want to explore some of the coastline or beach hop you can look into renting a dinghy.

Best of Henley Cay and Caneel Bay Adventure

Enjoy the Best of Henley Cay and Caneel Bay Kayak, Hike & Snorkel Adventures "combined" into a 5 hour tour with a picnic lunch! Henley Cay is among St John's most colorful snorkeling destinations. See coral gardens, schools of tropical fishes and marine life at this deserted island. Seabirds soar overhead and feed nearby. Explore the Caneel Bay Peninsula. Kayak turquoise waters, hike Turtle Point Trail and snorkel to see turtles and sting rays. Look for deer, wild donkeys, mongoose and hermit crabs. Departs daily from Virgin Islands EcoTours' Honeymoon Beach Hut. Book online or call toll free.

Caneel Bay Kayak, Hike & Snorkel Adventure

Listen to our guests! We are ranked #1 in Trip Advisor: "Best Experience on St. John", "Do it early in your trip", "Amazing Adventure", "Great family activity", "Learn and have fun exploring St. John!", "Very interactive tour of the islands unique ecology with a great staff.", "Don't miss this!". Kayak on turquoise waters, hike along scenic Turtle Point Trail and snorkel over coral reefs and see colorful fish, turtles and sting rays. Consider upgrading to a 5 hour tour with lunch: The Best of Henley Cay and Caneel Bay! Limited availability, reserve early. Book online or call us toll free.

Eco Hike & Snorkel Tour: Lind Point to Honeymoon

Explore the best of VI National Park above and below the water. Depart from the Visitor Center in Cruz Bay and hike the Lind Point Trail. Learn about flora, fauna, cultural and historical trivia along the way. At Honeymoon Beach your guide will teach you to snorkel and identify the colorful sea life. The final portion of your hike takes you through a grove of wild cinnamon, the botanical gardens of Caneel Bay Resort and the ruins of a Sugar Plantation. Perfect for wedding, corporate and private groups. Book online with Virgin Islands EcoTours or call toll free.

Honeymoon Beach All-Inclusive Watersports Daypass

Experience St John's most romantic beach with the All-Inclusive Day Pass that includes: snorkel gear, life jacket, lounge chair, pool float, kayak, standup paddle board and locker. Enjoy island time in a hammock! Snorkel with sea turtles! The Honeymoon Hut sells cold drinks and souvenirs with food available. Taxi to Caneel Bay and walk 8 minutes to Honeymoon Beach or hike the Lind Point Trail from Cruz Bay. Perfect for wedding, corporate and private groups. $49 per adult and $10 per child. Book online using promo code VINOW for 10% discount or call toll free.

SUP-St. John Explore St. John on a Paddleboard!

St. John with its warm, turquoise water is the perfect place to learn to paddle. After a 2 hour lesson with our ISA-certified SUP Instructors you will have mastered the basics of Stand Up Paddling and are safe to go and explore St. John waters on your own. If you have paddled before and know what you are doing, you can also rent a paddleboard from us! We have a wide variety of high quality Fanatic SUPs for rent. No matter what your size or weight, we will have the right board for you. Weekly board rental includes complimentary delivery to your villa!

Rent Kayaks, SUP, Snorkel Gear & Pool Floats

FREE DELIVERY to your rental villa or campground! Includes a trolley, foam car top carrier, kayak back rests, SUP leash, lifejackets, paddles, cable and lock! The kayaks are single and double easy-to-paddle-at-on-top-kayaks. Single kayak $145 per week, Double kayak $165 per week, SUP Standup Paddleboard $165 per week, Snorkel Gear $30 per week, pool float $45 per week! The lowest prices, largest variety, best service and newest gear available seven days a week! Must have beach toys for exploring the VI waters! Book online with Virgin Island Ecotours or call toll free 1.877.845.2925

Henley Cay Kayak & Snorkel Adventure

Henley Cay is one of St John's premier snorkeling spots! Kayakers and snorkelers love the challenge of a 20 minute paddle across Caneel Bay from Honeymoon Beach to Henley Cay, part of the VI National Park, a UNESCO Biosphere Reserve. The protected beach is fringed with colorful coral reefs teeming with schools of vibrant fish and marine life. Flocks of seabirds fly overhead and feed close-by. Consider upgrading to a 5 hour tour with lunch: The Best of Henley Cay and Caneel Bay! Perfect for wedding, corporate and private groups. Book online using promo code VINOW for 10% discount or call us toll free.

Cruz Bay Watersports

We have PARASAILING, WAVERUNNERS, DINGHY RENTALS and more! Go parasailing and experience the thrill of flying high above the brilliant blue waters of the Caribbean. Enjoy the breathtaking views the Virgin Islands have to offer. On a waverunner tour you will pilot your own personal watercraft on a half hour tour and see the islands like never before. Or rent a dinghy and be your own captain! Set course and see secluded beaches and pristine bays on your own schedule. Half and full day dinghy rentals are available. Must be 18 years or older to operate waverunner and dinghy. Visit our website for more information.   /

Other Activities in St John

Dining St. John, Virgin Islands

Restaurants on St. John offer you various levels of enjoyable dining experiences. From casual outdoor dining to five course meals on patios over looking moonlit Cruz Bay, you will enjoy it all. Experienced chefs create mouth-watering entrees, often offering a large selection from continental cuisine to French, Italian and Caribbean foods

Featured Dining

Mathayom Private Chefs St. John Catering

Gourmet Drop-Off makes life a little easier by offering a large selection of fresh creations for dinner and breakfast. Whether you are just arriving or have had a long day on the water, it is one less thing to worry about. For a little more pampering consider a Private Chef. Formal or casual, our team will come to your location, set up your dining area, and serve you a one-of-a-kind menu. Each event has a unique bill of fare that has been customized for you. Visit our website to view past menus and get a feel of the food we produce. Allow yourself to truly relax while on vacation, contact us today!

In quaint Cruz Bay there are several narrow roads forming a small grid. Along these roads are several restaurants. There are a few restaurants right on the water. They offer pleasant ocean breezes and a great view. A short walk into Cruz Bay and you will find more restaurants offering everything from causal dining with BBQ chicken wings and beer to shrimp appetizers and steak dinners.

Cruz Bay is not the only area beckoning to your taste buds to enjoy its restaurants; you can also head out to Coral Bay for some causal and fun dining.

If you want a more formal dining experience the resorts on the islands have great restaurants that you can go to or there are several fabulous spots on the hillsides around Cruz Bay.

Other Dining

Name	Location	Phone
Asolare	Caneel Hill	(340) 779-4747
Banana Deck	Cruz Bay	(340) 693-5055
Caneel Beach Terrace	Caneel Bay Resort	(340) 693-6111
Cafe Concordia	Salt Pond Bay	(340) 693-5855
Deli Grotto	Mongoose Junction	(340) 777-3061
Fish Trap	Cruz Bay	(340) 693-9994
High Tide Bar & Seafood Grill	Cruz Bay	(340) 714-6169
La Tapa	Cruz Bay	(340) 693-4199
Lime Inn	Cruz Bay	(340) 779-4199
Mango Deli	Westin Resort	(340) 693-8000
Morgan's Mango	Cruz Bay	(340) 693-8141
Skinny Legs	Coral Bay	(340) 779-4982
Waterfront Beach Bistro	Cruz Bay	(340) 777-7755

St. John Beach Guide

Most visitors and locals will agree that when it comes to beaches on St. John a 'good to best' scale just would not do. The scale for describing St. John's beaches is 'Great', 'Greater' and 'It's a secret so I am not telling anyone'. All beaches on St. John are open to the public. Beachfront property however, in many cases is private and a few popular beaches have hotels nearby. Respect private property when accessing beaches. It is illegal to collect shells from beaches in the Virgin Islands; shells are confiscated at airport customs. There are no clothing optional beaches in the Virgin Islands

St. John Nightlife & Entertainment Guide

St. John is a small island with a very small island feel. The population is small, welcoming and friendly. St. Johnians like to 'hang out', have a drink, exchange stories and listen to music. If 'chilling out' is your type of ambiance than you will enjoy the small bars and open air 'watering holes' of St. John.

The nightlife on St. John tends to be more low-key then its sister island St. Thomas. Outings are a friendly affair. There are several bars around the island. Many focus on music, food and good times. Live music, including reggae bands, is a popular entertainment. Some very colorful bars can be found in Coral Bay. Cruz Bay is also home to several entertaining spots. It is not unusual in Cruz Bay to find people gathered in front of a small bar, sitting almost on the road drinking, talking and having a great time.

For a quieter more romantic night out on St. John have a nice dinner, desert and drinks at a great restaurant. There are several to choose from.

If you are staying at one of St. John's resorts you will find that there are several bars, lounges and restaurants at the resort; and that these places offer evening entertainment and an opportunity to mingle with locals and other visitors.

St. John from time to time has live performances including plays and concerts. During special holidays like Christmas and Carnival there are often great events to attend

Shopping on St. John, Virgin Islands

Shopping on St. John is unique and fun. Casual and entertaining shopping areas are in Cruz Bay and Coral Bay. These two areas are the primary "towns" if anywhere on St. John can really be considered such. Quaint tropical buildings and gorgeous stone Caribbean structures house small stores that sell an assortment of items. Shops and boutiques on St. John are well known for unique items like hand made jewelry, local crafts, paintings and pottery

VItraders.com

You can shop online for your favorite souvenirs, travel guides and maps from the Virgin Islands. VItraders.com has been serving customers for over 14 years. Planning a vacation and need a guide book, beach guide, map or bird watching book? VItraders.com has a great book section. Are you looking for souvenirs like wall calendars, cook books, Caribbean dolls, coloring books, hot sauce, magnets, postcards, mugs, Christmas Cards and ornaments, hats or shot glasses? You will find a nice selection of all of those and more. Click over to VItraders.com for Virgin Islands Books and Souvenirs.

In Cruz Bay, the main "town" and shopping area, you will find shops at Mongoose Junction, along King Street and at Wharfside Village – all are in walking distance from the ferry dock. A casual walk through Cruz Bay and you will find swim wear, bags, liquor, jewelry, art work and more – all in a delightfully calm and casual environment.

Mongoose Junction attracts the eye; it's a beautiful piece of art in itself and it houses many fantastic stores with fascinating items; handmade pottery, paintings, jewelry and even hand painted clothing! Get great deals on beautiful gold earrings and necklaces and pick up unique souvenirs.

Shopping Hours on St. John

Mongoose Junction

Normal hours: 10am to 5pm 7 days a week. A few stores open earlier (9am) or close later (8pm). During slow season and on weekends some shops close.

Cruz Bay is a small area so restaurants and bars are all in the same vicinity as the shops; making a break for lunch or a drink easy.

Shops in Coral Bay offer an assortment of t-shirts and souvenirs. Great restaurants are mixed in with the shops – making shopping, having lunch and beach time a great and easy way to spend the day.

Resorts on St. John also offer shopping. Boutiques on hotel grounds offer an assortment of books, sundries, handicrafts, sportswear, sunglass, watches and souvenirs.

Shopping on St. John is great fun; shops are individualized and unique. Walking through shady alleys, having a break on a beach front veranda or cool courtyard and purchasing special gifts is what it's all about. Happy Shopping!

Getting to St. John (from St. Thomas)

Ferry Boat

Whether your vacation is on St. John or you are visiting St. Thomas and want to head over to St. John for the day – you will be taking a boat to travel between the two islands.

Things to Know

1. St. John does not have an airport. Travelers must fly into the Cyril E. King Airport on St. Thomas (airport code: STT) and then continue to St. John by boat.

2. You can travel between St. Thomas and St. John using a public ferry or a car barge; how to directions on taking both

are available below. You can also travel between St. Thomas and St. John by private water taxi/boat..

3. There are two ferry departure points on St. Thomas for the passenger ferry to St. John; one is in Charlotte Amalie and the other is in Red Hook.

4. There is a ferry terminal in Charlotte Amalie that is used for ferries going to the British Virgin Islands. The ferry from Charlotte Amalie to St. John does not leave from that terminal.

5. The car barge from St. Thomas to St. John departs only from Red Hook.

6. Once in a while people confuse St. John (the island in the Virgin Islands) and St. John's (the capital city in Antigua). Antigua is a different Caribbean island, not part of the USVI, and it is 210 miles away from St. John. Mixing them up can be a pricey mistake if you have to change your flight or cancel hotel reservations. So remember the island in the USVI is St. John (no s).

How to take the Passenger Ferry
From St. Thomas to St. John
Step 1: Choose a ferry: Charlotte Amalie to St. John; or Red Hook to St. John. The Charlotte Amalie ferry is closer to the Airport (about 3 miles; 10 minute drive in low traffic); and also to the Cruise Ship Docks (about 1.5 miles; 7 minute drive in low traffic). The Charlotte Amalie schedule has 3 departures a day. There is no terminal, the ferry picks up right off the Charlotte Amalie waterfront. The Red Hook ferry is about 10 miles from the airport, about a 35 minute drive in low traffic, and about 8-9 miles from the Cruise Ship Docks. The Red Hook ferry has departures every hour on the hour from early morning to midnight. There is a ferry terminal in Red Hook with benches and a small bar. Reservations are not required for

either ferry. Check the Ferry Schedule for more details, ticket prices, and schedules.

Step 2: Get to the ferry. So you've chosen which ferry you want to take; now you need to get there probably from the airport, cruise ship dock or your hotel. You should try to be at the ferry at least 15 minutes before departure. You can take a taxi, rent a car and drive yourself or try public transportation. If you are at the cruise ship dock and taking the Charlotte Amalie ferry, you could walk; it's about 1.5 miles and would take about 30-35 minutes. If you are driving yourself; there is a paid parking lot in Charlotte Amalie called Fort Christian Parking Lot – it's a short 2-3 minute walk from the ferry. And if driving to the passenger ferry in Red Hook there is a paid parking lot at the Red Hook Ferry Terminal. If it's full there are a couple paid parking lots on the hillsides across the street.

Step 3: Buy your tickets. For the Charlotte Amalie ferry you buy the tickets from the crew once the ferry arrives. For the Red Hook ferry you buy the ticket at the terminal. You can purchase a one way ticket, or round trip. There is a surcharge for luggage. Credit cards are not accepted; cash only.

Step 4: Board the ferry. Hand your ticket to the ferry attendant, get on the ferry and enjoy the ride. The ferry boats have enclosed seating on the main deck, and open air seating on the top deck. From Charlotte Amalie to St. John the ferry ride takes about 35 minutes. From Red Hook to St. John the ferry ride is about 15 minutes.

Step 5: Arrive in Cruz Bay, St. John. From there you can explore Cruz Bay on foot. Take a taxi to visit the island. There is a taxi stand at the end of the ferry dock. You can walk to a car rental company and rent a vehicle. If you are staying on St. John and your hotel or villa representative is meeting you – they will usually meet you near the end of the ferry dock.

From St. John to St. Thomas

Step 1: Select a departure time. Ferries depart from Cruz Bay Ferry Dock. Check the Ferry Schedule to select the departure time that works for you. Arrive at Ferry Dock at least 15 minutes prior to departure.

Step 2: Buy tickets. If you already have your ticket, proceed to the waiting area. If you need a ticket there is a ticket booth; specify whether you want a ticket for the Red Hook or Charlotte Amalie ferry. The waiting area is covered and gated; an attendant opens the gate when the ferry is ready for boarding.

Step 3: Board the ferry. Hand your ticket to the ferry attendant, get on the ferry and enjoy the ride. You may want to double check with the attendant collecting the ticket that you are boarding the correct ferry (to Red Hook or to Charlotte Amalie).

Step 4: Arrival in St. Thomas. If your destination is Red Hook and you need a taxi, there is a taxi stand at the Red Hook Ferry terminal. If your destination is Charlotte Amalie, there are typically taxis in the area.

How to take the Car Barge
From St. Thomas to St. John
Step 1: Choose a departure time. The car barges depart from Red Hook on St. Thomas to Enighed Pond, St. John. There are three companies that operate car barges. Check the Ferry Schedule page for more details, ticket prices, and schedules.

Step 2: Drive to Red Hook. The car barge and passenger ferry terminal are right next to each other; each has its own entrance.

Arrive about 25 minutes prior to departure time. There is a port tax of $3 per Car, small SUV, Motorcycle; $4 per truck, van, large SUV. The port tax is paid to an attendant in a booth just at the entry area for loading on the car barge.

Step 3: Waiting area. An attendant in the car barge loading area will typically ask what barge you plan to take; and instruct you on where to place your car. Wait in your car until the barge is ready to be loaded.

Step 4: Boarding the car barge. The barge attendants will direct driver's onto the car barge, and indicate where to park on the barge. You will reverse your vehicle onto the car barge.

Step 5: Buy tickets. Once on the barge, you can either stay in your car, or you can get out and sit on the upper deck. An attendant will approach you at your car, or on the deck, to sell you a ticket. You can purchase one way or round trip. No credit cards, cash only. A receipt will be provided; and the return ticket if you purchased a round trip fare. Be sure to ask if the return ticket can be used on another barge. There are three companies operating car barges; two of them accept each other's tickets. Also confirm the return times – usually they are printed on the receipt.

Step 6: Enjoy the ride over. If you are sitting on the deck, start heading back to your car once you get close to the dock area in St. John. The arrival place is Enighed Pond, just outside Cruz Bay.

From St. John to St. Thomas
Step 1: Choose a departure time. There is only one departure point for the car barge to St. Thomas, and that is Enighed Pond. There are three companies that operate car barges. Check the Ferry Schedule page for more details, ticket prices, and schedules.

Step 2: Drive to Enighed Pond. There is an attendant outside the loading area that will ask you which car barge you intend to take; or if you already have a ticket they might ask to see the ticket so they can direct you to the correct car line for that barge.

Step 3: Boarding. Wait in car line until the attendant directs the line to start moving toward the barge. You will reverse your vehicle onto the car barge. The attendant will instruct you on where to park on the barge.

Step 4: Buy tickets. Once on the barge, you can either stay in your car, or you can get out and sit on the upper deck. An attendant will approach you at your car, or on the deck, to sell you a ticket or collect your existing ticket. You can purchase one way or round trip. No credit cards, cash only. A receipt will be provided; and the return ticket as well if you purchased a round trip fare. Be sure to ask if the return ticket can be used on another barge. There are three companies; two of them accept each other's tickets. Also confirm the return times – usually they are printed on the receipt.

Step 5: Enjoy the ride over. If you are sitting on the deck, start heading back to your car once you get close to the dock area in Red Hook, St. Thomas.

Getting Married on St. John, Virgin Islands

Does your dream wedding take place on a secluded beach? How about at sunset with steel pan music playing? Or perhaps on a sailboat! Whatever your tropical dream wedding entails, it can be arranged on St. John. Ceremonies can be elaborate or simple. Perhaps you'd like to have your wedding at Annaberg Plantation, Hawksnest Beach or a gazebo overlooking the beach. St. John provides a truly amazing location for saying "I do". Spend your honeymoon on St. John in a private villa or be pampered at a resort.

Honeymoon Beach Weddings & Wedding Parties
Honeymoon Beach is St John's premier beach destination your wedding party will never forget! Caneel Bay Resorts wedding planners coordinate with Virgin Islands Ecotours to arrange an unforgettable wedding bash with beach rental, ordained minister, tented bar, a kayak filled with ice and beer, live music, BBQ lunch, homemade gelato ice cream, beach attendants, hammocks, restrooms, gift shop, picnic tables, beach games, lots of shade and all day beach fun with lounge chairs, multi person party floats, kayaks, SUP and snorkel gear for everyone! Plan the best for your friends and family for groups up to 250! Call Virgin Island Ecotours for more information.

Mathayom Private Chefs ~ St. John Catering
Whether your wedding or banquet is formal, casual, assisted, family style, cocktail, or buffet we will work with you to make your special function memorable for every guest. We can do Asian, Caribbean, Italian, Vegetarian or a menu theme based around your party. Our most common requests are for our Caribbean Beach BBQ and our Island Fancy Menu. Enjoy them as they are or alter them to suit your individual needs. Equipment rentals are also available for a smooth all-inclusive dining experience. For more information visit our website or contact us by phone or email.

Island Style Weddings
The Caribbean has captured your heart! Sugar white sand, tranquil breezes and turquoise waters are calling you. We are here to guide you, partner with you and to share all of our island expertise. We want to design the perfect Caribbean celebration that reflects your style and personality. Your Island Style Wedding is your first statement as a married couple. Let us help you make your vision a reality. This is your day and we would be honored to be a part of it.

Island Bliss Weddings

One of the most innovative wedding planning services in the US Virgin Islands, Island Bliss Weddings has helped couples plan intimate ceremonies for those that wish to elope to elegant wedding weekends for those that want to celebrate with all their family & friends in our beautiful tropical islands. We understand it can be a little stressful to plan from so far away, it is our goal to make sure that our couples arrive without a worry in their heads! We take care of each detail and make sure your day is executed flawlessly, so you all you have to do is enjoy your time in the islands and begin your new lives together with a heart full of love and smiles.

Ceremonies of St. John

Congratulations on your engagement! Say, "I Do" on a pristine white beach, in plantation ruins, in a luxury villa, on a private yacht, or in one of the oldest churches in the Caribbean. Our staff has years of experience in planning unique island weddings. Ceremonies of St John is the first wedding planning company located on St. John. We know you have a unique expression of your love and we are here to convey your vision. Consider us your friend on St. John and allow us to design your special day.

Crown Images

Sage Hammond specializes in destination weddings and is based in the Virgin Islands. She has quickly become one of the most sought after professional photographers in her region. Sage has a vibrant contemporary fine art approach to wedding photography that gives her images a unique look. Please visit her website for additional information and rates.

Wedding Consultants

A wedding consultant based in the Virgin Islands is your best resource for planning your wedding. Whether the consultant is affiliated with a hotel or is in private business their knowledge of island weddings will make everything so much easier for you. Hotel packages might run anywhere from $550 up to $3000+. Prices depend on the package and can include the basics; a great location and the minister or can include bouquets, cake, photographer, champagne, limo, crystal flutes, videographer and live music.

Private consultants can arrange your wedding basically anywhere you choose but often will suggest the areas that are best suited for such an event. Packages can be basic to elaborate with prices around $300 and up. A consultant can take care of everything for you; processing the license, getting a great photographer, flowers, cake, caterers, transportation and if necessary even witnesses! They will insure that your day is extra special, just the way it should be!

The Virgin Islands are perfect for anniversaries and renewing vows! Consultants can plan these events as well and make it extra special for just the two of you or for the whole family. Contact a local wedding consultant and start planning your island dream wedding or vow renewal.

If you are planning to arrange the wedding yourself you will find wedding license information for the USVI below.

REQUEST MARRIAGE LICENSE APPLICATIONS

The marriage license application fee is $200 ($100 for application fee and $100 for the license). There is an 8 day waiting and processing period, which can be waived depending on circumstances. The application is good for 1 year. Court marriages in front of a judge are performed on weekdays by appointment and will cost around $200. Religious ceremonies should be arranged directly with church officials. If either party has been divorced, a certified copy of the divorce decree must be presented. If you are requesting a marriage license through the mail, without the help of a local wedding consultant you will have to pick up the license yourself on arrival. This can only be done of regular business days.

St. Thomas /St. John
Superior Court of the Virgin Islands
P.O. Box 70

St. Thomas, USVI 00804
Telephone: (340)774-6680

St. Thamos

Attractions

Charlotte Amalie, St. Thomas
Charlotte Amalie beckons you to stroll along her cobble stone alleyways, climb her streets of steps, admire antique West Indian furnishings in historic homes and explore 17th century Danish fortifications. Founded in 1681 by Danish settlers, it contains a wealth of buildings that provide a glimpse into colonial life. It is listed in the National Registry of Historic Places as an area of particular historic interest. Often referred to as Downtown or just Town, Charlotte Amalie today is a bustling center for government, schools, offices, shopping and residences! Visit old and new Charlotte Amalie; see the evolution from a colonial trading post to one of the busiest duty free ports in the Caribbean! Here is a selection of sites you might visit.

Charlotte Amalie is divided into three quarters: Kongens (King's) Quarter, Dronningens (Queen's) Quarter and Kronprindsens (Crown Prince's) Quarter. They share similarities like the use of step-streets, but each has a unique character. All three quarters contain historically significant buildings. Some of the best preserved and most accessible are located in a small area of Kongens Quarter, and in the commercial area along Main Street in Dronningens Quarter.

Night Kayak in the Mangrove Lagoon
Looking for a really unique adventure? Then you will love our Night Kayak Adventure with Pirate and Ghost Stories. From Blackbeard, Bluebeard, and Teach, prepare for an experience with a dash of

history, a pinch of the macabre, and a spooky twist when you kayak along the dark and winding waterways of the Mangrove Lagoon. Enjoy the starlit sky as you look for stingrays, tarpon, and other marine life illuminated with lights below your kayak. You will go back in time and relive those days when pirates, ghosts, and jumbies still roamed the islands. Hear tales of shipwrecks and the eerie legends that haunt the islands to this day.

St. Thomas Parks, Reserves and Historic Places

Enjoy nature and history while vacationing in St. Thomas! Swim among colorful reef fish and turtles, kayak through beautiful mangrove forests while keeping an eye out for a graceful egret, hike to historic sites, take photos, join a boating excursion, or snorkel! Several areas on and around St. Thomas are protected or designated as parks allowing wildlife and plant life to have a secure habitat; and in some cases giving you an opportunity to explore it all. Included are watershed and mangrove lagoon systems, small islands and cays, beaches and marine areas. Various historical treasures are also protected.

Bird Island at Sunset by Kayak in Mangrove Lagoon

Enjoy an unforgettable sunset paddling quietly through a bird sanctuary in St Thomas Mangrove Lagoon. Visit an egret and pelican rookery at Bird Island and paddle through a winding maze in the shallow waters of a submerged mangrove forest. An Expert Nature Guide will guide you on a peaceful paddle through the dynamic Benner Bay estuarine ecosystem and St Thomas East End Reserve's. Discover the diversity of birds that inhabit this Mangrove Lagoon Wildlife Sanctuary and Marine Reserve. Enjoy this rare and unique way to experience a romantic tropical experience.

Activities

St. Thomas: Learn to Sail

The waters around St. Thomas are beautiful, the weather fabulous, the trade winds perfect – perfect for sailing! And not just any sailing, YOU sailing. That's right, while visiting St. Thomas you can take sailing classes that give you the know how to sail a 20 foot sailboat and larger boats with more advanced classes. You can even do an excursion where you actively participate on a racing yacht as you and your team head toward a finish line – sounds exhilarating doesn't it?

Island Tour by Taxi

The most popular way to take a tour of the island is by taxi. Many of them use vans or open air safari buses. They will include popular sites and scenic look out points. Some tours include a combination of shopping, sightseeing and a couple hours at the beach. Customized tours are available too. If you want to head to St. John your tour will start with a boat ride to Cruz Bay, St. John and then will continue with a safari taking your around to popular spots. Visit the Featured Tours below for more information.

Air Force 1 Fun Tours

Call (800) 501-0122
Call (340) 774-8342
Call (340) 690-8080

St. Thomas Shopping, Island Tours and Beach Trips! We offer great island tour packages which include visits to the most exciting sites on St. Thomas. Air Force 1 Fun Tours are St. Thomas' friendliest, most fun tours on the island. Visit Crown Mountain for stunning views of the west side of the island, Mountain Top, Skyline Drive for the world famous view of Charlotte Amalie harbor and enjoy your choice of Magen's Bay, Coki Beach or Sapphire Beach. Please visit our website for more information, pricing on tours or for transportation to and from a beach.

Mr. Nice Guy Taxi & Limousine Service
Call (786) 296-8767

At Mr. Nice Guy we provide more than just your basic car service. We provide Taxi, High End Limo and luxury transportation services to get you to your final destination in style. From Airport services, Private Jet, Private Yacht, Villa/Resort pickups, hourly service, events and much more. We at Mr. Nice Guy Taxi & Limousine will make sure your trip is first class all the way. When passengers need to travel in style they call Mr. Nice Guy Taxi & Limousine Service because people with taste never settle for less than luxury. Make your reservations and book your ride NOW!!!

St. Thomas & St. John Tour Company
Call (800) 679-6501
Call (340) 513-8535

St. Thomas and St. John Tour Company offers unsurpassed excursions in the Virgin Islands! We are a full service tour and taxi company. We offer island tours, historical sightseeing, beach and snorkeling excursions. Our tour services are affordable, customer focused, and suitable for all - from families to groups of 300 people. The Virgin Islands are some of the most beautiful islands in the world with pristine white beaches, turquoise water and tropical foliage. We have a lot of fun here, and are happy to call it home. Come and explore our islands with us! Email and chat with us today.

Islander Taxi Service Inc.

Come and be amazed by the history, culture and natural beauty that exist in the landmarks, beaches and across our beloved island. Hear the history and learn about our island. Let us be your guide as you explore. Whether you are interested in indulging yourself to your hearts content by shopping in the Shopping Capital of the Caribbean on Main Street, basking in the sun and taking a dip in the crystal blue waters or taking an island tour; Islander Taxi Service Inc. is committed to making that vision become a reality. Contact us today!

Flamon's Taxi & Island Tours
Call (340) 513-4041

Get the most enjoyment possible on your visit to St. Thomas with an island tour organized by certified tour guide Bruce "Chicago" Flamon. In 2013 Bruce won the VI Hotel and Tourism Association's Tommy Star Award for Taxi Driver of the Year! Take a scenic driving tour, shop for a couple hours and visit beautiful beaches! Join a standard group tour; or take a private tour. On private tours you can plan the itinerary and explore at your pace. Pick up and drop off downtown, at your ship, hotel or the airport. Small and large groups welcome. Contact us today.

The popular taxi vehicle used for island tours is called a safari. Its a truck which has been outfitted with bench seating in the back. It is open air but covered. Safari buses vary in size, some can hold up to 26 passengers, for this reason these tours are often group tours. Private tours can be requested or arranged and there are smaller vans, SUVS and cars that serve as taxis as well.

Taxi rates, including taxi tours, are set by the VI Taxicab Association. Examples include: Sightseeing Tour for 2 hours; one passenger $50, two or more passengers $25 per person. Tour for 3 hours; one passenger $60, two or more passengers $30 per person. When you choose exclusive, customized tours expect to pay more than the standard rate.

St. Thomas: Powerboat Rentals & Charters

Rent a powerboat, and plan your own itinerary; stop at a few snorkeling spots, have a nice picnic on a deserted beach or a fun trip to a neighboring island. Boats include; 25-28' Makos, 25' Boston Whalers, 26' Prowler Catamarans, 24' Island Daysailers, among others. Rentals are usually equipped with iceboxes, so you can travel with food and drinks. Boat rental operators will advise you of good locations to visit and provide you with maps and directions. They prefer you have some experience with navigating a boat and some require knowledge of local waters. Captains are available if necessary for an extra fee, usually around $80 for ½ day and $115 for a full day. Prices range from around $280-$650 for ½ day rentals and $385-$700 for a full day, in addition to fuel consumed. Prices vary based on type and size of boat

Island Wilson Excursions
Snorkeling - Sightseeing - Island Hopping - Whatever. Let Capt Wilson take you on an unforgettable trip aboard his incredibly smooth riding 30ft power catamaran, Deja Blue. Experience the pristine beaches, colorful reefs and tropical vistas of the Virgin Islands in stretch out comfort.
Call (340) 626-2583

Lion In Da Sun
Lion In Da Sun uses a 28ft Scout powerboat providing stability, speed, and open bow seating while island hopping on a day trip. Discover what the area is known for; snorkeling, beachside restaurants and bars and white sand beaches. Visit the BVI islands of Jost Van Dyke and Norman Island or head to the Baths for the day. Stay in U.S. waters and see all of what St. John has to offer in the bays and cays surrounding the island. Ultimately the entire trip is up to you; we are however more than pleased to help you design it and then boat you to the best day of your vacation!
Call (340) 626-4783

Alternate Attitude

The most breathtaking of adventures! The most competitive rates! A customized daylong excursion on Alternate Attitude will be the highlight of your Island memories, whether you snorkel with the turtles of Maho Bay, pub-crawl to Willie-T's and Foxy's, or explore our top-secret secluded beaches that only the most experienced captains know. Alternate Attitude is an eco-friendly 27' Pro-Line go-fast boat with twin Mercury 225 engines and a comfortable layout for up to 6 guests. Our wildly popular, affordable adventures fill up quickly, so book now! Remember the fun you had, not the bill afterwards!

Call (340) 690-8747

Call (713) 817-3898

Alternate Attitude

Beach Bum Boat Rentals

Don't just "rent a boat"... have the best day of your vacation! We have the largest selection and widest variety of stylish and comfortable boats for rent on St Thomas & St John. Large group? We can accommodate up to 32 people on one boat! Swim with turtles, rays and dolphin, lay on white sand beaches, sip a Painkiller in a hammock at the Soggy Dollar Bar, and enjoy the spectacular beaches of the U.S. & British Virgin Islands. Your captain will customize the perfect day for you. Flexible cruise ship schedules. Reserve your day early, we book up fast!

Call (855) 550-8728

Take It Easy

What do Brad Pitt, Kenny Chesney, and Cate Blanchett all have in common? They have all cruised on Take it Easy! Explore the islands in luxury! The day is yours! Whether it's with family, friends, a wedding party, or private getaway; you will surely enjoy the crystal blue waters and the warm Caribbean sun on TAKE IT EASY. This

luxurious 45' Sea Ray can accommodate up to 12 passengers in comfort and style. Visit our Facebook page at www.facebook.com/pages/Take-It-Easy-VI or our website for more information. Check out our excellent reviews on Trip Advisor!
Call (340) 677-1320

Nauti Nymph Power Boat Rentals
Nauti Nymph Powerboat Rentals has been voted the number one Powerboat Rental by readers of the Daily News and consistently receives the highest ratings. It is the largest and one of the longest established powerboat rental companies. The boats are beautifully appointed Fountains and Everglades. 29 to 35 feet, equipped with large bimini tops, ice chests, upholstered seating and all required safety gear. Your itinerary can include any destination between St. Thomas, St. John and Virgin Gorda in the privacy of your own boat. Nauti Nymph will assist with your itinerary for a bareboat or captained daytrip. For reservations: 1-800-734-7345. Website: www.nautinymph.com.
Call (800) 734-7345
Call (340) 775-5066

Elixir Charters
Elixir, a sixty foot custom Hatteras Motoryacht is the largest and finest day charter yacht in the Virgin Islands. Allow us to pamper you with an eggs benedict breakfast and filet mignon and lobster tail lunch served to you at a bronze sea turtle table on our shaded aft deck. Enjoy three fabulous snorkel/beachfront stops, top quality snorkel gear, double kayak, fast inflatable, double hammock, giant sun pad, air conditioned salon with Bose home theater system, and our open top shelf bar including vintage wine and champagne. Full day trips and sunset dinner cruises daily. BVI trips available on private charters. Unforgettable!
Call (340) 344-3336

Vilocity Boat Rentals

Your day, your way. We make suggestions, you decide the location and pace. From remote beaches, caves and hikes; to the more popular bars, restaurants and beaches. The local's choice for good reasons: our 33 x 10 foot power-boats are wide, roomy and stable in high seas. They feature twin 225 Yamaha outboards, a large Bimini top, built in coolers, shower, changing room, dry gear locker, plugin for your music device and snorkel gear. All this at reasonable rates and with some of the most knowledgeable and entertaining captains the islands have to offer. See us on Facebook and TripAdvisor!
Call (340) 677-0739

VIBE Charters

Welcome aboard VIBE Charters and our beautifully appointed 26 foot Glacier Bay Power Catamaran, VIBE 1. VIBE 1's stable platform, comfortable seating, fuel efficient engines and knowledgeable captain will transport you to your destination in style. Are you are craving a snorkel adventure in the stunning waters of the US or British Virgin Islands? Or simply a fun filled day of island hopping and sampling the wide variety of local beaches, restaurants and beach bars? Let VIBE Charters take you away from the ordinary and into the extraordinary! After all, It's Not Just Another Boat Ride!
Call (340) 626-2875

One Love Charters

Experience the British Virgin Islands and the U.S. Virgin Islands the way the locals do! Book with One Love Charters and you'll be able to visit all the destinations the VI has to offer... Including the ones you can't read about! Whether you want to snorkel beautiful reefs, bar hop beach to beach, or just relax on the boat with an ice cold beverage in hand, One Love Charters will work to make your day with us the highlight of your vacation!

Call (340) 227-5229

See and Ski Powerboat Rentals

See and Ski is the choice for chartering a boat by the St. Thomas/St. John community. The fleet features 26' Prowler Cats, powered by fuel efficient and reliable engines, equipped with full biminis for extensive shade coverage, coolers, ample dry storage and freshwater showers for your comfort. Known for their smooth, dry ride, the twin hulls take all sea conditions easily. Island Hop, Beach Bar it, Fish, Dive, Spearfish or Snorkel. Checkout is streamlined. Your itinerary is individual to make it your day! Best Captains in the VI - experienced, knowledgeable & FUN! Explore, play, see & ski, the beauty of the Virgin Islands!

Call (866) 775-6268

Call (340) 775-6265

Magic Moments Luxury Excursions

Explore the most beautiful destinations in the British and US Virgin Islands with the day charter company that was voted number ONE by readers of the Daily News and was awarded the Certificate of Excellence by Trip Advisor. This is a true, all inclusive luxury day excursion that takes you to the best destinations in the US and British Virgin Islands. Your yachts of choice are 45' Sea Rays or a 52' Sunseeker. Elegant cockpit space for lounging and dining,beautifully appointed interior , full bathrooms. French style continental breakfast, gourmet lunch with lobster ettouffee, chilled prawns, Caribbean chickensalad, homemade desserts, open bar.

Call (800) 734-7345

Call (340) 775-5066

Sonic Charters

Sonic Charters offers private custom day trips to the U.S. and British Virgin Islands on 32' Intrepid and 33' Jupiter center console power boats. Whether you want to party the day away or lay back and unwind, we want to make it happen! With comfortable seating for up to 9 and capacity up to 12, Sonic Charters can provide unsurpassed luxury for a fun filled day. The USVI and BVI are an open canvas to explore and our local captains can take you to places other companies won't! We look forward to spending the day with you!

Call (340) 244-5096

Call (203) 889-6003

Captain Nautica

Seeing the USVI and BVI is an experience of a lifetime! Captain Nautica has what it takes to make it even better! Plan your own trip or let us make suggestions. Up to 12 guests will be able to enjoy our 41' Bravo motorboat with twin-engine Yamaha outboards that will get you as far away as Virgin Gorda or Culebra. We also have 31' RIB motorboats available. All our boats feature a shaded Bimini top and the tour includes captain, gas, drinks, music, snorkel gear, fresh-water shower and, of course, water, sand and fun!

Call (340) 775-9360

Caribbean Blue Boat Charters

AFFORDABLE PRICING for Families & Friends! Rent a Private Boat w/Captain! Our Stylish 36ft Marlins provide a most comfortable ride. Feel the wind as you cruise the islands. Listen to Buffet, Reggae or your choice from our 12 speaker surround sound. Your Day, Your Way! Snorkel w/ turtles, rays & tropical fish. Visit Trunk Bay St. John, Turtle Cove, The Baths, Virgin Gorda, Jost Van Dyke, or relax on a beautiful beach. Call us today to help design an unforgettable trip! All things are possible! Includes seating up to 12ppl, snorkel gear & bathroom. Our Captains are FUN & experienced. Visit TripAdvisor/Facebook. Call or Text, we book up fast!

Call (340) 690-2583

St. Thomas Boat Rental

Home of the $99 gas guarantee with the most professional crew in the islands. Pick from a variety of private charters boats legally certified for up to 12 passengers. We have boats for every budget starting at $450. Call for details (813) 465-2665 or visit stboat.com.
Call (340) 227-5144

In Theory Charters

In Theory is the perfect charter for relaxing or having an active, adventurous, fun filled day. This 40ft trawler offers day charters to the U.S. & British Virgin Islands. She is spacious and comfortable. One of the nice things about our boat is that the boat itself has a lot of room to wander around. Our trips range from swimming with turtles, to exploring ship wrecks, or hanging out on a deserted island. We would love to organize and plan your special event, birthday, wedding or cruise ship excursion. We donate $15 from each charter to a community organization; we appreciate your support and pay it forward.
Call (340) 677-0050

St. Thomas: Eco-Tours

The Virgin Islands' beaches, coral reefs, historic ruins and forest provide endless hours of exploration and enjoyment on St. Thomas, as well as inspiration and opportunities for reflection. Visitors can enjoy a variety of activities on the land and in the water. Some visitors explore the on their own, while others prefer a guided tour. Tours include a guide that describes the history and ecology of the area as well as pointing out and interpreting the flora and fauna as you go along.

Hassel Island Kayak, Hike & Snorkel Adventures
Call (877) 845-2925
Call (340) 779-2155

Adventure to the VI National Park's premier historic site! Depart from Frenchtown, and kayak through Charlotte Amalie's harbor to Historic Hassel Island and explore America's most intact British Naval Forts. Careening Cove has centuries of importance housing British Barracks, ship repair facilities, coaling stations and a US Naval Base. The Creque Marine Railway had a multimillion dollar facelift. Snorkel over a coral reef at a deserted beach. Consider upgrading to a 5 hour tour with lunch! Limited availability, reserve early. Book online or call us toll free.

Mangrove Lagoon Kayak, Hike & Snorkel Adventures
Call (877) 845-2925
Call (340) 779-2155

A unique, guided, multi-eco experience awaits you! This award winning tour takes guests of all ages and experience levels kayaking in the Mangrove Lagoon. Explore a mangrove forest and try your luck with a hermit crab race. A short walk along a coral and shell beach brings you to impressive volcanic cliffs, tidal pools and the famous Red Cliffs Blow Hole! Snorkel in a clear shallow lagoon. Guided tours depart daily: 5 hours w/ lunch, 3 hours, and 2 1/2 hours. Perfect for wedding, corporate and private groups. Book online with Virgin Islands EcoTours or call toll free.

Coral World Ocean Park
Call all (888) 695-2073
Call (340) 775-1555

Spend the day at Coral World Ocean Park and get up close and personal with the beauty and magic of Caribbean marine life in a stunning setting. Learn about life on a coral reef from the unique Undersea Observatory and about local conservation efforts in one of our interactive presentations. Pet a shark, hand feed a stingray or a rainbow lorikeet! There are several gift shops, cafes and shower facilities. Additional activities include Sea Lion activities, Sea Trek Helmet Dive, Snuba Diving, Shark and Turtle Encounters, and the Nautilus Semi-Submarine. Located next to Coki Beach. Open 9-4 daily, November - May. Summer schedule will vary.

Night Kayak in the Mangrove Lagoon
Call (877) 845-2925
Call (340) 779-2155

Looking for a really unique adventure? Then you will love our Night Kayak Adventure with Pirate and Ghost Stories. From Blackbeard, Bluebeard, and Teach, prepare for an experience with a dash of history, a pinch of the macabre, and a spooky twist when you kayak along the dark and winding waterways of the Mangrove Lagoon. Enjoy the starlit sky as you look for stingrays, tarpon, and other marine life illuminated with lights below your kayak. You will go back in time and relive those days when pirates, ghosts, and jumbies still roamed the islands. Hear tales of shipwrecks and the eerie legends that haunt the islands to this day.

Bird Island at Sunset by Kayak in Mangrove Lagoon
Call (877) 845-2925
Call (340) 779-2155

Enjoy an unforgettable sunset paddling quietly through a bird sanctuary in St Thomas Mangrove Lagoon. Visit an egret and pelican rookery at Bird Island and paddle through a winding maze in the shallow waters of a submerged mangrove forest. An Expert Nature Guide will guide you on a peaceful paddle through the dynamic Benner Bay estuarine ecosystem and St Thomas East End Reserve's. Discover the diversity of birds that inhabit this Mangrove Lagoon Wildlife Sanctuary and Marine Reserve. Enjoy this rare and unique way to experience a romantic tropical experience.

Attractions on St. Thomas, Virgin Islands

Your vacation is booked and now you are wondering about sightseeing and what to do in St. Thomas? You can explore some of the parks and reserves by taking a nature hike, or on a kayak excursion. How about zip lining in St. Thomas? You can learn about fascinating marine animals at Coral World. There is the butterfly garden, tramway to Paradise Point, and the Botanical Gardens. Beautiful vistas are plentiful and an island drive makes seeing them easy. Head to the hills on St. Thomas island for a stop at Mountain Top; or down towards the sea to the capital of the U.S. Virgin Islands, Charlotte Amalie. Charlotte Amalie is filled with history -- old churches, historic houses, watch towers and a fort! It is also home to the winter wonderland, Magic Ice. Visit popular areas like Frenchtown and Red Hook for a lunch break, or a stroll. What are you going to see on your St. Thomas vacation?

Virgin Islands Ecotours
Call (877) 845-2925
Call (340) 779-2155

Every year Virgin Islands EcoTours receives Best of Awards such as: Kayak Tours, The Best EcoTour and Best Attraction by the readers of the VI Daily News. Kayak Hike & Snorkel Adventures are offered at three locations: St. Thomas Mangrove Lagoon; St. John Honeymoon Beach; and Historic Hassel Island. Professional guides lead ecological and historical tours where you kayak, hike and snorkel in one unforgettable adventure of fun and learning. VI EcoTours received the Certificate of Excellence by Trip Advisor. Wedding, corporate and private groups receive personalized service. Book online or call toll free.

Coral World Ocean Park
Call (888) 695-2073

Call (340) 775-1555

Spend the day at Coral World Ocean Park, one of St. Thomas's Greatest Attractions. Get up close and personal with the beauty and magic of Caribbean marine life in a stunning setting. View life on a coral reef from the unique Underwater Observation Tower. Pet a shark, hand feed a stingray or a rainbow lorikeet! There are several gift shops, cafes and shower facilities. Additional activities include Sea Lion activities, Sea Trek Helmet Dive, Snuba Diving, Shark and Turtle Encounters, and the Nautilus Semi-Submarine. Located next to Coki Beach. Open 9-4 daily, November - May. Summer schedule will vary.

Tree Limin' Extreme Zipline Park
Call (340) 777-9477

Soar through the rainforest on a gratifying 2 1/2 hour zipline canopy tour starting with a fun and exciting ride in a six wheel drive pinzgauer to the top of St. Peter Mountain. Be amazed by unbeatable views from eight aerial platforms, fly high above the forest on six exhilarating ziplines and soak up the sun on our breathtaking skywalks as our professionally trained guides lead you through the experience of a life time. Hang with us and you will also experience the only zipline of its kind in the Caribbean... the Yo-Yo! It's the only way to fly on the Island! Book online or call us!

Butterfly Garden
Call (340) 715-3366

Take flight at the Butterfly Garden. Enter a lush tropical botanical garden home to butterflies from around the world. During your 25 minute tour, knowledgeable guides will entertain you with fascinating facts about the extraordinary life cycle of these beautiful creatures as they change from eggs to caterpillars to butterflies through the miracle of metamorphosis. Wear bright colors and perfumed lotions to attract the butterflies to you! Double the fun and take a stroll through the outside botanical gardens showcasing a wide variety of local plants and butterfly species. Located next to the Cruise Ship Dock in Havensight. Open 8:30am-4:00pm daily. Summer Hours May-October will vary; please call.

St. Thomas: Animal Encounters

The Virgin Islands' are home to some neat and interesting animal life, many of which live in the beautiful ocean around the islands. Visitors to St. Thomas can get up close with some of these land and sea animals! Perhaps you want to feed an iguana or colourful birds, swim with a turtle, or how about pet a shark. That's right a shark. You can also swim with sea lions! Animal encounters include educational information and fun activities; a great combination that is sure to be a highlight of your vacation.

Coral World Ocean Park
Call (888) 695-2073
Call (340) 775-1555

Spend the day at Coral World Ocean Park, one of St. Thomas's Greatest Attractions. Get up close with the beauty of Caribbean marine life. Imagine a magical meeting with a playful sea lion. The Sea lion Swim and Encounter were created especially for you and the sea lions to share a series of thrilling activities while establishing a unique bond. Or, Join two of our rescued Green Sea Turtles or our Juvenile Sharks for an awesome experience. During your orientation learn about the biology of these beautiful creatures & the threats they face in the wild. A portion of the proceeds goes towards animal rescue and rehab efforts. #awesomeericavi

Bird Island at Sunset by Kayak in Mangrove Lagoon
Call (877) 845-2925
Call (340) 779-2155

Enjoy an unforgettable sunset paddling quietly through a bird sanctuary in St Thomas Mangrove Lagoon. Visit an egret and pelican rookery at Bird Island and paddle through a winding maze in the shallow waters of a submerged mangrove forest. An Expert Nature Guide will guide you on a peaceful paddle through the dynamic Benner Bay estuarine ecosystem and St Thomas East End Reserve's. Discover the diversity of birds that inhabit this Mangrove Lagoon Wildlife Sanctuary and Marine Reserve. Enjoy this rare and unique way to experience a romantic tropical experience.

Virgin Islands Ecotours
Call (877) 845-2925
Call (340) 779-2155

Every year Virgin Islands EcoTours receives Best of Awards such as: Kayak Tours, The Best EcoTour and Best Attraction by the readers of the VI Daily News. Kayak Hike & Snorkel Adventures are offered at three locations: St. Thomas Mangrove Lagoon; St. John Honeymoon Beach; and Historic Hassel Island. Professional guides lead ecological and historical tours where you kayak, hike and snorkel in one unforgettable adventure of fun and learning. VI EcoTours received the Certificate of Excellence by Trip Advisor. Wedding, corporate and private groups receive personalized service. Book online or call toll free.

St. Thomas: BVI Excursions

The British Virgin Islands (BVI) are made up of about 50 islands and islets. The four largest islands are Tortola, Virgin Gorda, Jost Van Dyke and Anegada. Tortola is the largest island with an area of 21 square miles. The other larger islands are Anegada at 15 square miles, Virgin Gorda at 8 square miles and Jost Van Dyke at 3 square miles. Smaller islands include Great Tobago, Peter, Cooper, Norman, Guana, Beef, Great Thatch and Marina Cay. The British

Virgin Islands are among the world's loveliest cruising grounds for charters and yachts. Take a day trip to the BVI and visit some of the top sights like the Baths on Virgin Gorda and picturesque Jost Van Dyke, it will be a vacation highlight!

Magic Moments Luxury Excursions
Call (800) 734-7345
Call (340) 775-5066

Explore the most beautiful destinations in the British and US Virgin Islands with the day charter company that was voted number ONE by readers of the Daily News and was awarded the Certificate of Excellence by Trip Advisor. This is a true, all inclusive luxury day excursion that takes you to the best destinations in the US and British Virgin Islands. Your yachts of choice are 45' Sea Rays or a 52' Sunseeker. Elegant cockpit space for lounging and dining,beautifully appointed interior , full bathrooms. French style continental breakfast, gourmet lunch with lobster ettouffee, chilled prawns, Caribbean chickensalad, homemade desserts, open bar.

VIBE Charters
Call (340) 626-2875

Welcome aboard VIBE Charters and our beautifully appointed 26 foot Glacier Bay Power Catamaran, VIBE 1. VIBE 1's stable platform, comfortable seating, fuel efficient engines and knowledgeable captain will transport you to your destination in style. Are you are craving a snorkel adventure in the stunning waters of the US or British Virgin Islands? Or simply a fun filled day of island hopping and sampling the wide variety of local beaches, restaurants and beach bars? Let VIBE Charters take you away from the ordinary and into the extraordinary! After all, It's Not Just Another Boat Ride!

See and Ski Powerboat Rentals
Call (866) 775-6268

Call (340) 775-6265

See and Ski is the choice for chartering a boat by the St. Thomas/St. John community. The fleet features 26' Prowler Cats, powered by fuel efficient and reliable engines, equipped with full biminis for extensive shade coverage, coolers, ample dry storage and freshwater showers for your comfort. Known for their smooth, dry ride, the twin hulls take all sea conditions easily. Island Hop, Beach Bar it, Fish, Dive, Spearfish or Snorkel. Checkout is streamlined. Your itinerary is individual to make it your day! Best Captains in the VI - experienced, knowledgeable & FUN! Explore, play, see & ski, the beauty of the Virgin Islands!

Lion In Da Sun
Call (340) 626-4783

Lion In Da Sun uses a 28ft Scout powerboat providing stability, speed, and open bow seating while exploring the British Virgin Islands. Discover what the area is known for; snorkeling, beachside restaurants and bars and white sand beaches. Visit Tortola, Norman Island, Cooper Island or mini islands like Sandy Spit and Sandy Cay; grab a drink or two at quintessential beach bars like Foxy's and Soggy Dollar on Jost Van Dyke; or head to the Baths for the day. Ultimately the entire trip is up to you; we are however more than pleased to help you design it and then boat you to the best day of your vacation!

Take It Easy
Call (340) 677-1320

What do Brad Pitt, Kenny Chesney, and Cate Blanchett all have in common? They have all cruised on Take it Easy! Explore the islands in luxury! The day is yours! Whether it's with family, friends, a wedding party, or private getaway; you will surely enjoy the crystal blue waters and the warm Caribbean sun on TAKE IT EASY. This luxurious 45' Sea Ray can accommodate up to 12 passengers in comfort and style. Visit our Facebook page at www.facebook.com/pages/Take-It-Easy-VI or our website for more information. Check out our excellent reviews on Trip Advisor!

Caribbean Blue Boat Charters
Call (340) 690-2583

AFFORDABLE PRICING for Families & Friends! Rent a Private Boat w/Captain! Our Stylish 36ft Marlins provide a comfortable ride. Feel the wind as you cruise the islands. Listen to Buffet, Reggae or your choice from our 12 speaker surround sound. Your Day, Your Way! Snorkel w/ turtles, rays & tropical fish. Visit The Baths, Virgin Gorda, Soggy $ Bar, Foxy's, Jost Van Dyke, Willy T's Pirate ship or relax on a beautiful beach. Call us today to help design an unforgettable trip! All things are possible! Includes seating up to 12ppl, snorkel gear & bathroom. Our Captains are FUN & experienced. Visit TripAdvisor/Facebook. Call or Text, we book up fast!

St. Thomas: Jet Ski Rentals and Tours

So you want to get out on the water for some high power fun on your own personal watercraft? How about heading out with a guide to explore some near shore snorkeling spots and to check out the beauty of the island along its coastlines? Jet Ski rentals are available on St. Thomas in single and double riders at various beaches. Jet ski tours are available and often include sightseeing along the coast and in some cases stopping at beaches or at snorkeling spots.

340 Water Sports
Call (340) 690-3390

Welcome to 340 Water Sports- The ultimate Virgin Islands jet ski experience. 340 Water Sports at Bolongo Bay Beach Resort is your #1 choice for exhilarating and carefree fun for individuals and groups! Join us on one of our three jet ski riding options to ride the waves and explore the waters of paradise. Contact us today!

St. Thomas: Golf & Tennis

Golf: The Virgin Islands are home to four golf courses, one of which is located on St. Thomas. There are no golf courses on St. John or Water Island.

Mahogany Run Golf Course

Mahogany Run, opened in 1980, is a challenging course designed by George and Tom Fazio. There are 18 beautiful holes laid out on a 6,022 yard, par-70 championship course in a lovely valley overlooking the Atlantic Ocean. The most well known holes at Mahogany Run are the 13th-15th. They make up the spectacular "Devil's Triangle". So challenging are these three holes that anyone that plays all three without a penalty stroke is awarded a special certificate! Informal scratch tournaments go on throughout the year where visitors can play against local players. Mahogany Run is open to the public and is accommodating to hotel and cruise ship guests. Groups are welcome and special tournaments with prizes can be arranged. The pro shop is fully stocked with brand name merchandise including Ashworth, Izod, Monterrey Club, Callaway and Gear. Quality rental clubs are available.

Herman E. Moore Golf Course

There are no holes or facilities at the Herman E. Moore Golf Course. The course is located at the University of the Virgin Islands and is open to the public. It is used by golfers to practice putting and driving.

Golfing Events

Golfing events and tournaments are scheduled by different groups throughout the year. Visit the Events Calendar for more information.

Tennis

Tennis can be enjoyed at several locations on St. Thomas, mostly at resorts and hotels. Hotels/resorts charge non-guests for use of tennis courts and require reservations. Prices vary by resort. Some resorts offer private lessons

Resort/Condo Properties Facilities	Public Courts Facilities
1. Bluebeard's Castle Hotel 2. Bolongo Bay Beach Club 3. Mahogany Run Tennis Club 4. Marriott Frenchman's Reef & Morningstar Resort 5. Ritz Carlton 6. Sapphire Beach Resort 7. St. Thomas Yacht Club 8. Wyndham Sugar Bay Resort	Public courts are located in Subbase. Lights are turned off at 8 pm.

St. Thomas: Fishing

Amazing experiences await anglers in St. Thomas! Go offshore fishing in pursuit of Marlin, Sailfish, Dolphin Fish (Mahi-Mahi), Wahoo and Tuna. Or try your luck getting a bite and reeling in some Kingfish, Barracuda, Bonito, Jacks or Yellowtail Snapper while inshore fishing.

Wondering when the best time of the year is to come to St. Thomas and haul in that big catch you can go home and talk about for years! The short answer is that some species are around all year and others have peak seasons. Fishing charter operators and captains are knowledgeable about the islands' waters and seasons. They can provide information on what you might find on the end of your line when you go out fishing with them during your St. Thomas vacation.

Peanut Gallery Charters
Call (340) 642-7423

Are you ready to catch some fish and some memories! Captain David of Peanut Gallery Charters is enthusiastic about fishing and about helping you have a great time. Peanut Gallery is a 26' Prowler Custom Cat Sport Fishing boat and it is designed for your comfort and enjoyment. Charters are available for light tackle inshore sport fishing and deep sea sport fishing. Visiting by cruise ship; special packages and pick up at the cruise ship dock are available. Snorkeling and beach hopping can be incorporated if interested. For more information contact Peanut Gallery today.

Fishing charters in St. Thomas include inshore, offshore and marlin trips. A few charters offer trips starting at 2 hours, however the most common are ½ day trips (4 hours, typically between 8am and noon, or 1pm and 5pm); ¾ of a day (6 hours); full day (8 hours); and Marlin trips (10 hours, usually 7:30am to dusk). Short trips are generally inshore fishing only. Boat capacity of 4 to 6 passengers is common. Rates for fishing charters varies depending on length of trip, size of boat, inclusion of fuel in the rate versus fuel being a surcharge, and differences in services and equipment provided. Fishing charters generally have the details of their trips listed on their websites or can provide the information by email or telephone upon request. Explore your options; book a fishing trip and a have a great time!

Want to eat what you catch? Guests can generally request some of their catch, for example up to 20 lbs, the remainder stays with the boat. If you are interested in keeping some of your catch to take back to your vacation rental to cook be sure to ask about it. If you are staying in a hotel you can ask the captain for suggestions of restaurants close to the marina that will cook your catch for you!

If you are an avid fisher you might consider planning your vacation to St. Thomas around a fishing tournament. You can be a spectator or participate; some fishing charters are available for tournaments! Here is a sample: Memorial Day Tournament (May), Bastille Day Kingfish Tournament (July) and Wahoo Windup Tournament (November). The biggest of the fishing tournaments in St. Thomas is the USVI Open/Atlantic Blue Marlin Tournament (August).

For more information on fish species caught around the Virgin Islands including location, season and bait visit the Virgin Islands Fishing Guide and for regulations visit VI Fishing Regulations.

St. Thomas: Aerial Tours

Get a bird's eye view of St. Thomas and maybe the neighboring islands of Water Island and St. John on an aerial tour! Enjoy the thrill of flying, and the awe of experiencing the islands' beauty from above. Fly over Magens Bay, Charlotte Amalie and the lush West End of the island – admire it all. Aerial tours are available by seaplane, airplane and helicopter. Aerial tours are a fantastic way to see the islands.

Flying Fish Aviation
Call (340) 514-1680

Welcome to Flying Fish Aviation's Seaplane Tours! Your adventure begins boarding our boat at the Charlotte Amalie waterfront and motoring out to meet the Cessna 185 floatplane in the harbor. Soon you'll be skimming the waves and flying by the sights on Water Island, the West End, secluded little bays on the North side, gorgeous Magens Bay, and views of St. John and the British Virgin Islands. Upon splashing back down in the harbor, enjoy a leisurely boat ride back to the seawall. Scheduled Tours depart every half hour. Call to schedule your tour or build your custom tour today!

St. Thomas: Sailing Charters & Excursions

Enjoying the magnificent waters around St. Thomas will be the highlight of your vacation. Sail into small quiet coves, snorkel at beautiful reefs and just bask in the delightfully warm sun and tropical breezes. Or take a sunset sail and enjoy the tranquil beauty and romance of Caribbean evenings. Many sailing charter boats are 6-packs, holding a maximum of 6 passengers. There are larger boats that can accommodate groups. Charters are available in half day trips, full day, sunset sails, dinner cruises and also overnight trips or Term Charters. While in the Virgin Islands you can also Learn to Sail. Prices on day trips average around $85 to $125 a person, depending on charter and length of trip. Amenities vary but might include open bar, lunch, snorkel gear, floats and other water toys. Visit the featured charters below!

Featured Sailing Charters

Sail Wasabi
Call (340) 344-5429

Come sail aboard one of the most unique charter catamarans in the Virgin Islands. WASABI is a Stiletto 27 performance catamaran that specializes in fast, fun day sails. We sail the beautiful waters around St. Thomas and St. John. We explore the many beautiful anchorages, white sand beaches, off island cays, and coral reefs. We offer full & half day adventures with an open premium bar, deli style lunch with an array of choices, and premium snorkel gear and flotation. Let Captain Eric, a local Virgin Islander, be your guide and take you on a sailing adventure today.

Scubadu
Call (340) 643-5155

Scubadu is a 43 by 25 foot luxury Catamaran, specializing in private day, sunset, and/or dinner sailing excursions. Leave the crowds behind as you explore the beautiful waters, islands, and beaches of the U.S. Virgin Islands. We sail to beautiful snorkel and swimming spots you can't get to by car. Scubadu departs from Red Hook, St. Thomas or Cruz Bay, St. John. Because we only do private charters for a maximum of 12 people, we can customize your trip to your groups' needs. We provide the Captain, first mate, delicious food, beverages, snorkel gear, and fresh water showers. All you need to bring are towels and non-spray sunscreen.

New Horizons Daysails
Call (800) 808-7604
Call (340) 775-1171

Come aboard! Sail away with us for a day, and experience the perfect balance of adventure and relaxation aboard our sixty-four custom ketch. There is nothing like it! All you need is your towel! Swim, snorkel, sun or just relax as you sail the Caribbean in the unparallel spaciousness of your own private luxury yacht! There is no need to lift a finger; our warm, friendly, professional crew will pamper and entertain you. After all, it is your day! Call us to make a reservation for what will be the highlight of your trip!

Independence
Call (340) 775-1408

Spend the best day of your vacation aboard Independence, a big, comfortable ketch, cruising the bays of St. John and the small islands in Pilsbury Sound. She is equipped with awnings for shade, mats for sunbathing, top notch snorkel gear and all US Coast Guard required safety equipment. Captain Pat Stoeken has been delighting guests with sea stories, delicious meals, beverages, great sailing and snorkeling for over 20 years. A limit of 6 guests and a crew of 2 make for a personalized experience. Half or full day. Let us know what we can do to make a special day for you.

Fury Sailing Charters
Call (340) 643-7733

SWIM WITH THE TURTLES SNORKEL/SAIL. Join the crew aboard the newly refurbished sailing yacht FURY for a 3.5 hour excursion to the National Marine Wildlife Refuge at Buck Island. Here you will encounter endangered Green Sea Turtles and a variety of sea life in their natural habitat. Day Sail on St. Thomas includes: snorkel gear, open bar, snacks, fresh water shower and free pickup and drop off at the Havensight Cruiseship Dock. Trips depart twice daily and can accommodate up to 25 guests. Voted #1 excursion activity on St. Thomas by Tripadvisor.com. Sunset sails available. Don't miss this very unique and popular wildlife excursion!

Daysail Fantasy
Call (340) 775-5652
Call (340) 513-3212

Join Captain Pam with a maximum of just six guests on her modern Pearson sloop for an exhilarating sail in the protected waters of the beautiful St. John National Park and surrounding cays. Fishing, sailing, amazing snorkeling, beachcombing, swimming with endangered sea turtles and a deliciously prepared hot lunch in the shaded cockpit. Open bar & Jimmy Buffet tunes. Snorkel gear provided, along with special floats and instruction, making it easy for all ages. Just $140 per person all inclusive. Voted Best Daysail St.

Thomas 5 Years, Recommended By Trip Advisor, Frommers & Fodors.

Sail Island Girl Yacht Adventures LLC
Call (340) 344-4285

Come Sail Away aboard Island Girl, a 45 foot sloop! Maximum of 6 guests insures an intimate sailing and snorkeling adventure. Tradewind sailing at its best! Snorkel the pristine turquoise waters of the sunny Caribbean. Swim with sea turtles, rays, an abundant variety of sea life, corals, sponges, Caribbean fish, or even see a ship wreck. Havensight Dock arrival, we meet you where your ship docks, no taxi ride necessary. Crown Bay Dock arrival, a short taxi ride, approximately 5 minutes will get you to us. Captain Mike will whisk you away for your Caribbean Adventure! Half Day $75.00 pp, Full Day Sails $125.00 pp, Sunset Sails $65.00 pp.

Catania Yacht Charters
Call (340) 514-1231

Come Sailing with Catania Yacht Charters: excursions in the USVI and BVI, specializing in small groups of up to 6 guests. Catania is a traditional 80 year old sloop with a legacy of spending over 30 years circumnavigating the globe. Be pampered on an unforgettable excursion of a lifetime. Captain Ocean will enthrall you with the history of the Virgin Islands and stories of his around the world voyage. Discover pristine white sand beaches and enchanting hidden coves. Experience an underwater world full of spectacular marine life. Enjoy refreshments from our open bar. Full day, half day, and sunset sails available.

Tribal Daysails
Call (340) 998-7767

Tribal is a 40-foot trimaran specializing in custom tailored day charters, snorkel excursions, fishing, and sunset sails. The boat is a high performance racing trimaran designed for speed and comfort. The shaded cockpit can comfortably seat up to six guests for a more personal sailing experience. Hammocks and side nets also offer nice lounging areas to kick back right over the Caribbean ocean. Drinks and snacks are complementary all day. We also offer sunset sails. Experience a romantic sunset with an assortment of Hors d'oeuvres and a full open bar as you take in one of the most beautiful sunsets you will see in your lifetime. We specialize in sailing so make your reservation today!

Daydreamer & Coconut
Call (340) 775-2584

Have a fantastic day of great sailing, lots of snorkeling, excellent service and delicious food! Our boats offer speed which enables us to explore more of St. John and islands around her. Expansive decks, shade awning and floats satisfy your need for comfort. We try to take you off the beaten path to some of those places you've dreamt about. And whether its snorkel instruction, beverage and food service or just telling tales our amiable crew will help make your day memorable, safe and fun. We offer full and half day trips, sunset sails, Sunday brunch and BVI trips.

Its Amasing Charters
Call (340) 690-2735

Its Amassing is a brand new 2016 45 ft Lagoon catamaran that is all set to take you on your exclusive Virgin Island excursions. Leave the crowds behind as we take you to our special snorkel spots. Departs from St. Thomas' East End or Cruz Bay, St. John. We only do private charters; choose a daysail or an overnight stay. Your Captain is Hollywood Joe, he's been in these islands for over 40 years & makes sure you have the best food & drinks. We have plenty of snorkel gear, and offer fresh water showers. All you need to bring are towels, sunscreen and your sense of adventure!

Daysail High Pockets
Call (340) 715-2812
Call (340) 690-0587

A Cut Above! Join Captain Kathleen, a Registered Nurse and gourmet cook, for an outstanding day aboard the classic elegant yacht, High Pockets. Featuring spectacular sightseeing under sail, amazing snorkeling in secluded coves and just plain fun! Amenities include quality snorkel gear with expert instruction, sumptuous lunch and a thirst quenching open bar. Sailing St. Thomas, St. John and the Virgin Islands National Park with no more than six guests. Private parties welcomed. Wedding proposal, anniversary, birthday... we specialize in the celebration of great occasions and the everyday! Visit our web site for more information!

Goddess Athena
Call (340) 277-3532

Join us for unique adventures aboard our stunning, one-of-a-kind pirate ship! Queen of the Fleet for over 40 years, her 84 feet of classic lines make Goddess Athena a sight to behold. Friendly, knowledgeable crew, wonderful food and drinks, and sailing/snorkeling excursions tailored to your tastes will provide memories to last a lifetime. We invite you to experience the magic of sailing as only the pirates of the Caribbean knew. Our record 100% guest satisfaction speaks volumes. Join us today aboard the Goddess! Cannons by Request. Busty Wenches by Appointment Only. Sailing from Cruz Bay, St John.

Sail Eden
Call (340) 643-4388

Join Captain Bill and his lovely wife Christy for a wonderful, relaxing day of sailing and snorkeling on EDEN a 37 foot Tartan sailboat. Our first snorkeling location is Buck Island, a National Marine Wildlife Refuge. Explore coral reefs, snorkel over a ship wreck and see more beautiful fish than you can imagine. After a healthy snack we sail to Water Island and to Bill's secret cove for lunch, more snorkeling and beach exploring. Fabulous lunch/open bar/ shaded cockpit/ guided snorkeling tours (with instruction if needed). Departs from downtown St. Thomas. Six guests max. Half day tours $85 per person/Full day$135 per person $120 for children 12 and under.

Sail with Liberty Charters
Call (340) 690-4404

Sail with Liberty welcomes you aboard for a memorable full day sail, half day sail, or sunset sail among the tropical islands, cays, and reefs of St. Thomas and St. John National Park on our beautiful Bruce Roberts Offshore 44' ketch. Captain Ryan treats guests to a fun-filled day with amenities that include a delicious lunch, refreshing drinks, shaded cockpit, spacious decks, great snorkel and flotation gear, convenient swim platform, and terrific rates. TripAdvisor reviewers rank Sail with Liberty "Excellent." We also offer exclusive sails and special discounts (see coupon). See our video and more info at sailwithliberty.com.

St. Thomas: Scuba Dive

The underwater world in the Virgin Islands is stunning and truly amazing! Explore corals and gorgonian forest of sea fans and sea whips. Dive around caves, explore sunken boat wrecks or take a night dive and explore the fantastic world of nocturnal marine life! Swim among turtles, bright parrotfish, blue tangs, schools of fry and so much more.

The best conditions for diving in the islands are found during the summer and fall months, with visibility generally between 60 and 100 feet. Some sites, particularly in Pillsbury Sound, can be explored all year round as they are protected from the wind and rough seas that can affect other more open sites during the winter months. St. Thomas and St. John are close enough to each other that they share many of the same dive sites in the Pillsbury Sound area including Carval Rock, Congo Cay, Grass Cay, Mounds at Mingo, Arches and Tunnels of Thatch and Lovango Cay.

St. Thomas Diving Club
Call (340) 776-2381

Come join us at St. Thomas Diving Club and let us show you the incredible coral reefs, spectacular marine life and fascinating wrecks in our local waters. As a PADI authorized 5-star IDC facility, we cater to everyone from the beginning snorkeler to the experienced diver. PADI Training is our specialty. You will be led on your dive by one of our experienced instructors who will take you on a guided tour. St. Thomas Diving Club is located at the Bolongo Bay Resort on the beach next to Iggies. Contact us today to make reservations.

Coki Dive Center
Call (800) 474-2654
Call (340) 775-4220

Are you ready for the experience of a lifetime? You'll find it here! At Coki Dive Center, you'll have access to the best in beach and boat dives on St. Thomas. With expert lessons in Scuba and Snorkeling since 1989, you can count on the Coki Dive Center team for the experience of a lifetime from start to finish in a fun and safe atmosphere. We have expert PADI Discover Scuba Instructors and a Scuba adventure for the whole family. Let us help you create lasting memories with our Beach Diving, Boat Diving, Snorkeling and more!

Coki Dive Center

There are more than 40 moored dive sites around St. Thomas. Most are shallow dives and many only 15 to 20 minutes away from the shore/dock. Popular dive sites include WIT Shoal II, Navy Barges, Cow & Calf, Frenchman's Cap, Ledges of Little St. James, Cartanza Senora and Buck Island Cove. If you are a new or timid diver and rather not go offshore by boat to dive there are very good beach accessible sites, like Coki Beach and Hull Bay.

Dive operators are familiar with the various dive locations and can safely guide you to and around them. They can take you out for the first time, teach you to dive, get you certified and instruct you for higher levels of dive certification. An introductory course will run around $60 to $120. For the certified diver; two morning dives are around $75-$105, $65 to $95 for a night dive and wreck dives are around $130-$150. Certification course will run around $299-$400. Multi-day dive packages are also available for 4, 6...12 dives over several days. Whether you are a novice or a dive enthusiast, there is no better place to dive than in the warm, inviting waters around the Virgin Islands.

Scuba Diving Tips

1. There is an excellent recompression chamber in the Schneider Regional Medical Center on St. Thomas. It is on 24 hours a day.

2. Always check your equipment before each dive.

3. Never dive alone.

4. Enjoy the sites, but don't touch.

5. The survival of the underwater world depends largely on us; do not overturn rocks, kick up sand, pick up animals, touch coral. Be content with watching.

6. Leave the underwater world as you found it; future divers and the marine life will be happy you did!

7. Do not scuba dive if you are pregnant, too little is known about the effects of pressure on fetal development. Ask your doctor and/or dive professional for more information.

St. Thomas: Snorkeling & Super Snorkeling

From the new, never snorkeled before to seasoned snorkelers there is something for everyone. Rocky coast lines, near shore reefs, off shore cays and sunken items like ships and planes provide beautiful and varied snorkeling opportunities. The conditions are; great visibility, fairly constant water temperatures of 79-83 degrees year-round, calm seas with little current and fantastic underwater scenery. In other words, perfect for snorkeling. View gorgeous underwater gardens of coral and visit with the residents; turtles, rays, octopuses, moray eels and an abundance of fish large and small. With the use of a mask, snorkel and fins you can float on the surface and admire the marine life below. Snorkeling is an option from beaches and also by boat trips.

St. Thomas Diving Club
Call (340) 776-2381

Our afternoon snorkel trip goes to beautiful Buck Island and Turtle Cove. At Buck Island and Turtle Cove you are in a protected cove where the water is always calm and you are able to snorkel over a shipwreck and coral reefs. At both sites marine life is plentiful with lots of fish, turtles and rays. The afternoon snorkel trip departs from our dock at the Bolongo Bay Hotel at 1PM and returns before 5PM. All snorkel equipment is included and reservations are required. This trip is a perfect combination for both divers and snorkelers.

Mangrove Lagoon Kayak, Hike & Snorkel Adventures
Call (877) 845-2925

Call (340) 779-2155

A unique, guided, multi-eco experience awaits you! This award winning tour takes guests of all ages and experience levels kayaking in the Mangrove Lagoon. Explore a mangrove forest and try your luck with a hermit crab race. A short walk along a coral and shell beach brings you to impressive volcanic cliffs, tidal pools and the famous Red Cliffs Blow Hole! Snorkel in a clear shallow lagoon. Guided tours depart daily: 5 hours w/ lunch, 3 hours, and 2 1/2 hours. Perfect for wedding, corporate and private groups. Book online with Virgin Islands EcoTours or call toll free.

Hassel Island Kayak, Hike & Snorkel Adventures
Call (877) 845-2925
Call (340) 779-2155

Adventure to the VI National Park's premier historic site! Depart from Frenchtown, and kayak through Charlotte Amalie's harbor to Historic Hassel Island and explore America's most intact British Naval Forts. Careening Cove has centuries of importance housing British Barracks, ship repair facilities, coaling stations and a US Naval Base. The Creque Marine Railway had a multimillion dollar facelift. Snorkel over a coral reef at a deserted beach. Consider upgrading to a 5 hour tour with lunch! Limited availability, reserve early. Book online or call us toll free.

Coral World Ocean Park
Call (888) 695-2073
Call (340) 775-1555

Spend the day at Coral World Ocean Park, one of St. Thomas's Greatest Attractions. Get up close and personal with the beauty of Caribbean marine life in a stunning setting. Unique diving opportunities await you - Experience the thrill of exploring the ocean and all its wonders like a diver without the need for specialized training. Sea Trek is a guided walk on the ocean floor; the helmet provides the air, weight and stability to walk upright under the water. Want a diver's view of a coral reef, but not ready for scuba? Then try Snuba! A certified guide will lead you on your adventure.

From Beaches

Rocky coast lines and coral reefs near shore offer great opportunities to snorkel from beaches. Snorkeling from shore can be done with or without a guide. Some of the favorite beaches on St. Thomas for shore snorkeling include Coki Point, Sapphire Beach and Secret Harbor. View pictures and information on these and other beaches on the St. Thomas Beach Guide.

By Boat Charters

Charters for ½ or full day trips can take you out to two or three unique snorkeling areas. Many of the charters from St. Thomas sail or motor to protected marine areas in the Virgin Islands National Park on St. John. A favorite destination for day trips catering to cruise passengers is Buck Island National Wildlife Refuge on the south side of St. Thomas. Day charters often include lunch, drinks, snorkeling gear, a little history or stories by the captain and overall a combination of enjoying the weather, boating and snorkeling. More on Boat Charters

Tip: Don't snorkel alone. Don't touch or stand on coral, it is very fragile. Don't feed the marine life non-fish food. Cereal, cake, bread, nuts, dog biscuits, leftover hotdogs from lunch are not part of marine creature's natural diets and are considered unhealthy for them. Do wear sunscreen on your back or wear a t-shirt. You can easily spend 30 minutes to an hour floating along admiring the fish and that is plenty of time for the bright tropical sunshine to leave you with a painful sunburn.

The Gear

Fins, a mask and a snorkel. Some of the popular beaches have watersports booths that rent snorkel gear. You can also rent gear for a few days from a dive shop. A popular question by visitors is "Should I buy or rent a set". Frequent visitors agree that you should buy a set. Here's why. To enjoy snorkeling your gear needs to fit you well, particularly your mask. A leaky mask can ruin a snorkeling experience. When buying your mask test it out by holding it to your face without the strap behind your head and inhale slightly through your nose. Let go of the mask, it should say in place; this indicates a good seal. Your fins should fit you snugly when dry because when you get in the ocean the water acts as a lubricant. Snorkels are easier because they are mostly one size fits all. If you get a bag for your gear make sure its a mesh type bag so that water and sand can drain out. An underwater camera is a great accessory; you can pick up a disposable underwater camera at your local supermarket. Another neat accessory is a Fish ID Card; a small, waterproof card that includes popular marine animals you might see while snorkeling.

Super Snorkeling: For those of you who like snorkeling and are not divers there is a middle ground option called super snorkeling! Prices range from $57 a person to $99 respectively for the three different types of super snorkeling available on St. Thomas.

Snuba: Snuba enables people with the use of a mask and breathing tube attached to a tank of air floating on the surface to explore shallow coral reefs and marine environments while swimming under the water. Available to anyone from eight years old and up and doesn't require experience.

Helmet Dive: This form of super snorkeling involves divers wearing a helmet connected to the surface by an air hose. Divers climb down a ladder into the water, are fitted with the helmet and are off to explore a multitude of marine life. It is available at Coral World where it is called Sea Trekkin. Trekkers walk along a trail on the floor of the sea. A marine expert guides 8 people at a time around coral beds teeming with marine life. Available to anyone from eight years old and up and doesn't require experience.

Breathing Observation Bubble: This is an underwater scooter complete with a breathing and observation bubble attached to an air supply. You ride along on a scooter underwater while observing an assortment of beautiful marine life. Available to anyone from ten years old and up and doesn't require experience.

And say you want to enjoy the fascinating underwater world without getting wet, there are options for you too! How about a visit to an aquarium

Other Activities in St. Thamos

St. Thomas: Transportation: St. Thomas is not suitable for walking as a means of getting around and it is for the most part not hitch-hiking friendly. Exploring the island requires motored transportation.

Car Rental Information and Agencies: Renting a car will allow you to see the island at your own pace. Rental Agencies are located at the airport, walking distance from the main cruise ship dock and at large resorts. There are several agencies to choose from. Having your own transportation will make sightseeing, beach hopping, dining, shopping and exploring the island much more convenient. More Information on Car Rentals

Inter-Island Ferry and Air Service: Inter-island travel is facilitated by reliable ferry service and commuter airlines. Visit Virgin Islands Ferry Schedules and Inter-Island Air Carriers for more information.

Scooters, Motorcycles, Bicycles: There are a few shops that rent scooters on the island. Motorcycle rentals are not popular but a couple of the scooter rental shops do have them. Bicycles are available more for sport than transportation. Due to the mountainous nature of the island, using a bicycle to get around would really only be feasible for a serious athlete.

Taxis & Rates: Taxis are abundant and reliable. They are readily available at the airport, cruise ship dock, large resorts and at popular attractions and beaches. Taxis charge per person and by destination. There are no metered taxis. Taxi rates are are set by the VI Taxi cab Division. More Information on Taxis & Taxi Rates

Public Transportation: Country Buses travel between town and Red Hook every hour. They start running at 5.15am from town and end at 8.00pm from Red Hook. There are buses that travel past the airport toward Bordeaux. City buses travel between the Schneider Regional Medical Center bus stop to town starting at 6.15am until 8:00pm. The first bus from the Airport to town is at 6am and the last is 8:00pm. Country Bus Fare $1 and City Bus $.75. The public bus system is not very reliable so is not recommended for people on a tight or limited time schedule.

'Dollar Rides' or 'Dollar Taxis'
There are taxi drivers that run 'dollar rides' in safari buses. A safari is a truck that has been outfitted with bench seating in the back. It is open air but covered. Not all safari buses are 'dollar rides', some are regular taxis. The 'dollar rides' do not have signs identifying them as such; however they generally run the same route as the public bus and pull in or close to bus stops. If in doubt ask the driver before boarding. Also ask where they are heading to make sure they are going the route you want to go. They are for the most part un-regulated, and operate mostly to assist with the transportation

needs of residents. Some 'dollar ride' drivers charge non-residents regular taxi rates.

Dollar rides are $1 for short trips like: anywhere in town between the University of the Virgin Islands and the Hospital (Schneider Regional Medical Center), traveling to points between the Hospital and Pricesmart (supermarket), traveling from one point in the country to another (country is used to describe the middle and east end of the island). The fare is $2 for longer cross-island trips like: traveling from the Hospital to Pricesmart and beyond and traveling from Pricemart and beyond to anywhere in town.

Shopping on St. Thomas, Virgin Islands

St. Thomas is home to world renowned shopping! Hundreds of duty free shops line the streets and alleys of the capital, Charlotte Amalie. Multiple buildings in Havensight, where most cruise ships dock, house shops and boutiques. There are smaller malls around the island and even the larger hotels offer shopping!

The best buys on St. Thomas include jewelry, alcohol, china, crystal, perfumes, art, clothing, watches and cameras. If you are in the market for something in particular, primarily jewelry and cameras, it is a good idea to know what the going price is in your home town; some items are better deals than others so it pays to know what items cost at home.

Featured Shopping

VItraders.com
Call (340) 774-1181

You can shop online for your favorite souvenirs, travel guides and maps from the Virgin Islands. VItraders.com has been serving customers for over 14 years. Planning a vacation and need a guide book, beach guide, map or bird watching book? VItraders.com has a great book section. Are you looking for souvenirs like wall calendars, cook books, Caribbean dolls, coloring books, hot sauce, magnets, postcards, mugs, Christmas Cards and ornaments, hats or shot glasses? You will find a nice selection of all of those and more. Click over to VItraders.com for Virgin Islands Books and Souvenirs.

Caribbean Cowgirl
Call (340) 998-0858
Call (340) 998-9283

When shopping in Vendor's Plaza, make your first stop Caribbean Cowgirl. Located in space #6, we have been selling the finest, BEST quality STERLING SILVER jewelry since 1979. In business 36 years! Family owned and operated, we stand behind our products. Our unique pieces are designed by our very own Olympian Alayna Snell Kidd (Los Angeles, 1984 Games) and her cowboy husband. We specialize in the island ocean blue stone Larimar, hook bracelets, as well as different stones and shells. We have awesome lace and tie-dye clothing, great for the beach and as comfort wear. Credit cards accepted. Online shopping available, visit our website.

Gallery St. Thomas
Call (877) 979-6363
Call (340) 777-6363

Gallery St. Thomas, located in Palm Passage, is voted Best in the Virgin Islands for fine art and pottery. Take home beautiful artwork to remind you of your fabulous vacation. The gallery boasts the artworks of over 30 artists: from paintings in oil, watercolor and acrylic to pottery, turned wood, metal sculpture and jewelry. Our friendly knowledgeable staff can answer your questions and are happy to ship your purchases home. We have prices to meet every budget and a wide variety of small gifts including ornaments, maps, art prints, photographs and more. Please visit our website and check the show schedule for upcoming art exhibits, http://gallerystthomas.com/show-schedules/.

Shopping in Charlotte Amalie

The greatest density of stores is in Charlotte Amalie. The principal street there is Dronningens Gade, better known as Main Street. Parallel to Main Street is Back Street and Waterfront. Stores line each of these main roads, and in between the three roads are side streets and alleys where even more shops are located. In the alleys, like Royal Dane Mall, Palm Passage and Riise Alley, you will find many unique shops and boutiques. The stores in Charlotte Amalie are housed in and among historical buildings; so shopping and sightseeing in one trip is easy. Small cozy restaurants and a couple fun bars are located among the stores, perfect for lunch or a refreshing drink.

Charlotte Amalie Store Hours

Monday – Saturday, including Holidays: 9:00am – 5:00pm

Sunday Hours: While Sunday hours are usually half day, closing time 1:00pm; there are exceptions created by the number of ships in port. When there are no ships in port, some stores won't open at all. If there are several ships in port some stores might stay open until 3:00pm.

Note: Stores in Charlotte Amalie all unanimously close during the Children's and Adult's Carnival Parades. The parade route is along Main Street and the parades last all day. They usually take place during the last Friday and Saturday of April or the first Friday and Saturday of May. Visit the Events Calendar for more details on holidays and events.

Vendor's Plaza

In Charlotte Amalie there is an area called Vendors Plaza where vendors set up small booths, tables and tents from which they sell an assortment of souvenirs. Vendors Plaza is located across from the Emancipation Park and Fort Christian. There you will find silver jewelry, t-shirts, tropical print wrap skirts, shirts and dresses, imitation bags and watches, trinkets and more. There is also hair braiding, a photo op with a donkey, a coconut-for-sale stand, local food vendors and ice-cream stand.

Vendors Plaza is generally open Monday through Saturday from about 7:30am, when the vendors start setting up, until 5:00pm when they start packing up for the day. On Sundays, only a few vendors set up but this generally depends on the number of ships in port; more ships usually means more vendors.

Across the street from Vendors Plaza is a Co-op store that sells locally made crafts and goodies.

Shopping in Havensight
Havensight is the location of the second large agglomeration of stores that cater to visitors. It is right next to the primary cruise ship dock and the shopping area is made up of Havensight Shopping Center, Buccaneer Mall and Port of Sale. Long buildings house some 60+ stores. Shop for jewelry, clothes, perfumes, liquor, electronics, music, sunglasses, hot sauces and souvenirs. You can have lunch in Havensight also, there are several good restaurants to choose from.

Havensight Store Hours

Monday through Sunday, including Holidays: Hours of operation are 9:00am to 5:00pm, 7 days a week when there are cruise ships in port.

When no ships are in port hours are 10:00am to 3:00pm. On days when ships stay in port into the late evening; some shops remain open until 6:30pm.

Shopping Around the Island

Smaller shopping areas include; American Yacht Harbor in Red Hook, Lockhart Gardens, Tutu Park Mall and Nisky Center. These areas cater primarily to residents; you will find pharmacies, clothing stores, grocery stores, unique shops, art shops and music stores at these locations. Mountain Top and Paradise Point are both attractions, primarily known for offering extraordinary views but they both offer shopping as well. Tillett Gardens, is an oasis of arts and crafts; pottery, silk-screened fabrics, candles, paintings, jewelry, and more.

There are many options for shopping while visiting St. Thomas. There are lots of great stores, great items and great savings. Happy Shopping!

Duty Free Shopping – $1,600 Exemption

Applies to US residents returning to the US mainland

If you return directly or indirectly from a U.S. insular possession (which includes the U.S. Virgin Islands), you are allowed a $1,600 duty-free exemption. You may include 1,000 cigarettes as part of this exemption, but at least 800 of them must have been acquired in an insular possession. Only 200 cigarettes may have been acquired elsewhere. For example, if you were touring the Caribbean and you stopped in Jamaica, the U.S. Virgin Islands, and other ports of call, you could bring back five cartons of cigarettes, but four of them would have to have been bought in U.S. Virgin Islands.

Similarly, you may include five liters of alcoholic beverages in your duty-free exemption, but one of them must be a product of an insular possession. Four may be products of other countries. Duty free allowance on alcoholic beverages applies if you are 21 years old, it is for your own use or as a gift and it does not violate the laws of the state in which you arrive.

Travel to More Than One Country
If you travel to a U.S. insular possession and to one or more of the Caribbean Basin countries, for example, on a Caribbean cruise, you may bring back $1,600 worth of items without paying duty, but only $800 worth of these items may come from the Caribbean Basin country(ies). Any amount beyond $800 will be dutiable unless you acquired it in one of the insular possessions.

For example, if you were to travel to the U.S. Virgin Islands and Jamaica, you would be allowed to bring back $1,600 worth of merchandise duty-free, as long as only $800 worth was acquired in Jamaica.

Keeping track of where your purchases occurred and having the receipts ready to show the CBP officers will help speed your clearing customs.

Shopping Tips
a) Save your swimwear for the beach. It is considered taboo to wear swimsuits only or to walk about bareback anywhere but the beach or poolside. You will receive a much friendlier reception from sales people if you are covered up when walking around shopping areas and entering stores.

b) There are a lot of jewelry stores on St. Thomas. Many of the family run stores will bargain or haggle on the price, so be prepared to make offers lower than the original or ticket price. Larger stores also might give discounts but to a lesser degree, in any case its worth it to ask. Also if you have time then shop around, you might very well find the same item in another store.

c)   Say 'Good (Morning, Day, Afternoon)' to salespeople before starting a conversation. Locals are very greeting conscious and this small gesture goes a long way.

Getting Married on St. Thomas, Virgin Islands

A wedding on St. Thomas will be a magical beginning to your new life as husband and wife, or celebrate your anniversary with a vow renewal. Wedding planners are great resources, their knowledge of the island and weddings will make everything much easier for you. They can plan everything from simple to elaborate. You can also research your options and get in touch with wedding photographers, ministers, transportation providers, bakers, florists that are available and make arrangements on your own. If St. Thomas is going to be your wedding and honeymoon destination you'll want to consider the wedding/honeymoon packages some resorts on island offer!

Tropical Weddings VI
Call (340) 775-1087
Call (340) 998-0135

CONGRATULATIONS on your up-coming wedding. How exciting planning your wedding on a beautiful, tropical Island. Now that you have made your decision, please allow us to help you. With 30 years of Virgin Islands experience, it would be our pleasure to help you with every facet of your wedding from applying for your marriage license to waving good bye. Choose from a beautiful beach wedding, an elegant villa or perhaps getting married on the sea! We want to make sure that your wedding day is perfectly gorgeous, stress free, and that the planning is easy and fun, while keeping within your budget. I will be looking forward to hearing from you...

Weddings with Virgin Islands EcoTours
Call (877) 845-2925

Get married in America's paradise! As one of the top adventure companies in the Virgin Islands, all of our tours are also available for wedding ceremonies and wedding parties. Our ordained ministers perform ceremonies at Cas Cay in St. Thomas' Mangrove Lagoon Wildlife Sanctuary & Marine Reserve. Let us help you with planning, assist with food and drinks, everything from the pre-ceremony events, to the ceremony, to our award winning kayak, hike & snorkel adventures to experience the days before or after; and have an adventure you and your wedding party will never forget! Call Virgin Island Ecotours toll free 1.877.845.2925 for more information.

Sugar and Spice Salon Spa
Call (340) 776-5893

Sugar and Spice Salon Spa is the premier hair and beauty salon in the United States Virgin Islands serving St. Thomas, St. John, and St. Croix. Our award winning team, of expert stylists, specializes in bridal hair styling, airbrush makeup artistry, nail services, spray tans, lash extensions and more. Your beauty experience with the Glam Squad promises to be stellar whether on-location; at your villa, resort, condo; or inside our full service salon and spa located in Yacht Haven Grande. The best bridal stylists in the Caribbean are at your fingertips ready to create the work of art that is your bridal hair and makeup design.

Coral World Ocean Park
Call (888) 695-2073
Call (340) 775-1555

The only destination wedding location on St Thomas where you and your guests can get up close and personal with the splendor of the

Caribbean marine life! Combine your love for each other with your love of the environment in a beautifully unique tropical setting. Whether your dream wedding is an intimate day ceremony on land followed by fun adventures or a sunset wedding and reception with family and friends, Coral World boasts several magnificent venues for your special event. For the more adventurous Coral World offers underwater dive wedding packages that encompass Sea Trek and SNUBA. No certification required. Contact us for additional information.

Crown Images
Call (917) 655-7511

Sage Hammond specializes in destination weddings and is based in the Virgin Islands. She has quickly become one of the most sought after professional photographers in her region. Sage has a vibrant contemporary fine art approach to wedding photography that gives her images a unique look. Please visit her website for additional information and rates.

Wedding Transfers by Air Force 1 Fun Tours
Call (800) 501-0122
Call (340) 774-8342
Call (340) 690-8080

St. Thomas Weddings Transfers: Cruise Ship Dock, Hotel & Airport Transfers. We know that your wedding day is the most important day of your life and we want to help you make it even more special. Contact our specialists to discuss all your wedding transfer needs. Riding with us will enable you and your group to arrive at your wedding destination stress-free. If you are coming to St. Thomas for a wedding, corporate meeting or a family reunion and need to move a group from 2 to 350 to any location on the island we have vehicles to meet your needs. Visit our website for more information.

Island Bliss Weddings
Call (340) 514-2685

One of the most innovative wedding planning services in the US Virgin Islands, Island Bliss Weddings has helped couples plan intimate ceremonies for those that wish to elope to elegant wedding weekends for those that want to celebrate with all their family & friends in our beautiful tropical islands. We understand it can be a little stressful to plan from so far away, it is our goal to make sure that our couples arrive without a worry in their heads! We take care of each detail and make sure your day is executed flawlessly, so you all you have to do is enjoy your time in the islands and begin your new lives together with a heart full of love and smiles.

Marriage license information for the Virgin Islands is provided in the table below. In most cases wedding planners will assist with the marriage license application process.

MARRIAGE LICENSE APPLICATION

The marriage license application fee is $200 ($100 for application fee and $100 for the license). There is an 8 day waiting and processing period, which can be waived depending on circumstances. The application is good for 1 year. Court marriages in front of a judge are performed on weekdays by appointment and will cost around $200. Religious ceremonies should be arranged directly with church officials. If either party has been divorced, a certified copy of the divorce decree must be presented. If you are requesting a marriage license through the mail, without the help of a local wedding planner you will have to pick up the license yourself on arrival. This can only be done of regular business days.**St. Thomas / St. John**
Superior Court of the Virgin Islands
P.O. Box 70

St. Thomas, USVI 00804
Telephone: (340)774-6680

Weather

The year-round tropical savannah climate in the US Virgin Islands brings little temperature variation throughout the year. The islands' average summer temperatures of 82°F are scarcely warmer than the average winter temperatures of 77°F. Constant trade winds and warm sea water prevent temperatures from becoming too unbearably hot even during the heart of summer.

May rains briefly interrupt the typical end of December to early August dry season, but most US Virgin Islands rain falls during the mid-August to early December rainy season. Multiple showers during a single day are not uncommon during the US Virgin Islands rainy season. The US Virgin Islands are especially vulnerable to hurricanes during the wet season, when cruise ships are frequently forced to alter their schedule due to high winds or storms.

Best Time to Visit US Virgin Islands
Most US Virgin Islands visitors prefer to travel during the high and dry season, when crowds are at their highest and hurricane risks are at their lowest. Although hotel and airfare rates peak between mid-December and mid-April, those traveling in January can find quite a few discounts during the post-holiday season slump. February is the US Virgin Islands' busiest month of all.

Although many visitors want to avoid travel during the off season, especially to avoid risk of hurricanes between June and November, off season visitors can enjoy far fewer crowds and hotel rates slashed down to half of their high season prices. However, some restaurants and hotels may be under renovation or closed altogether during this low season.

Visitors who choose to travel to the US Virgin Islands during hurricane season should purchase advance trip cancellation insurance and be prepared for rerouting of cruise ships during high winds or rain storms. Not only is plenty of advance warning given before serious storms strike, even the locals pray to keep the storms away during Supplication Day, a legal July holiday. Another holiday, Hurricane Thanksgiving Day, celebrates the end of the year's hurricane season in late October.

Airports

Cyril E King Airport

Cyril E King Airport, named after the US Virgin Islands second elected governor, is situated on St Thomas southwest end. This airport, whose annual passenger throughput currently exceeds one million, is the busiest in all of the US Virgin Islands. Passengers from the mainland United States can fly non-stop to this airport from Charlotte, Miami, New York City, Atlanta, and Fort Lauderdale. There are also non-stop seasonal flights to and from Boston, Chicago, Minneapolis, and Washington, DC. Passengers can also fly directly to Puerto Rico, the British Virgin Islands, St Barthalemy, Anguilla, Antigua, St. Kitts, and St Maarten from this small airport. Staff who welcome arriving passengers with flavored rum may be Cyril E King Airports most unique passenger service, but the airport also features a tourist help desk, ATMs, a currency exchange, and the Hibiscus Cafe are among Cyril E King Airports passenger services. Passengers can also purchase jewelry and duty-free items here. Cyril E King Airport is the main air gateway to both St Thomas and the smaller island of St John, which has no airport of its own.

Hertz, Avis, and Budget all provide car rental at Cyril E King Airport, but passengers may find better car rental deals outside the airport as airport car rental dealerships often charge extra surcharges.

Most of the taxis parked on standby in front of Cyril E King Airport are large shared passenger vans transporting several passengers at once to various hotels, ferry docks, or other St Thomas locations. Charlotte Amalies central business district lies just two miles east of the airport.

Henry E Rohlsen Airport

This Virgin Islands airport named after Tuskegee Airman Henry E Rohlsen is the main air gateway to St Croix. Henry E Rohlsen Airport may be small, but its runway can accommodate aircraft as large as Boeing 747s. This airports non-stop flights to and from the mainland United States are year-round American Airlines flights from Miami and seasonal US Airways flights to Charlotte. Passengers can also travel non-stop to more than a dozen other Caribbean Islands, including St Thomas, from this airport. Henry E Rohlsen Airports passenger amenities include cafeterias, a currency exchange, a VIP lounge, and a tourist help desk.

Avis, Hertz, and Budget stand alongside three local car rental companies at Henry E Rohlsen Airport. The *St Croix Taxi Association* supplies public transportation which can easily travel the six miles to Christiansted or any other destination on St Croix.